SOLVING THE GRIM EQUATION

MORE GROWTH MEANS LESS FUTURE ON OUR DAMAGED PLANET

PAT DODD RACHER

Pat Dodd Racher
11/6/16

Published in the United Kingdom in 2015 by Cambria Books, Wales, United Kingdom

Original cover design © David Thorpe

Cartoon by Chris Madden

INTRODUCTION

Solving the Grim Equation considers how globalisation increases corporate power and marginalises communities, how fossil fuel use accelerates climate change, and why material standards of living will have to decline in all countries where populations use more than their fair share of natural resources.

Solving the Grim Equation continues the story begun in *Empty Plates Tomorrow?* which was published in 2007. The more we consume now, the less will be available to future generations, because continuous population growth and economic expansion on a finite planet are impossible. The dangerous consequences of the Fossil Fuel Age are apparent all over the planet and in the atmosphere above it.

The future of 'less' will be different but need not be the appalling dystopia which some predict. There are hopeful, if small, initiatives all around the world, and examples from Wales feature in this book.

The debt-laden global financial system is a colossal barrier because repayments of debt interest and capital require economic growth. The alternative is a depression in which populations are impoverished, unless governments agree debt cancellations with each other and plan for progressive reductions in energy use. Governments with the welfare of their populations at heart will also have to control the global banking industry, which contributes in no small way to the staggering wealth inequalities on this small planet.

The author is a graduate of the London School of Economics and lives in West Wales.

CONTENTS

LIST OF CHARTS

Currency conversions are at rates applicable in autumn 2014. Between then and spring 2015 the US Dollar appreciated by over 15% against the £ sterling.

Day of the Dead, Santiago Sacatapequez, Guatemala, when giant kites are flown in honour of the departed. This kite warns 'Calentamiento Global: Que Hemos Hecho?' – Global Warming: What Have We Done?

Powerful corporations still swat away protests: see 'Private Jets and Public Pittances' in Chapter 2, Globalisation: the Power to Colonise

Banana plantation owned by the US multinational Chiquita Brands International on formerly fertile land in the Motagua river valley, Guatemala. The bananas were encased in blue plastic, a sign of impregnation with the insecticide chlorpyriphos.

Agriculture for the benefit of others far, far away: see 'The Distress of Guatemala' in Chapter 2, Globalisation: the Power to Colonise

Organic vegetable growing at Alamar, La Habana del Este, Cuba. The co-operatively run farm or *organoponico* includes a wormery for improved compost and magnetised water for irrigation. Cuba has networks of organic urban farms, from which produce is sold to local people.

Access to land is crucial for future well-being: see 'Restricted Access to Land' in Chapter 4, Land and Food as Weapons

Stone pyramid among the ruins at Tikal, northern Guatemala. This is Temple V, 188 feet high. Tikal was abandoned by the Mayan people in the 9th century AD, probably the result of a population grown too large for the water and food supplies, both of which were depleted by prolonged drought.

Over-exploitation of resources leads to civilisation collapse: see 'The Distress of Guatemala' in Chapter 2, Globalisation: the Power to Colonise

Organic growing, as here in Alamar, Cuba, requires people, lots of people – but economic growth scenarios assume that numbers of rural workers will continue to decline.

Is this a wise assumption? See 'Cityworld' in Chapter 7, Tomorrow's Settlements.

Low-impact family home on the Rio Dulce, which flows into the Gulf of Honduras at Livingston, Guatemala. There are no roads in this part of Guatemala: the river is the highway.

Low-impact living is the way forward: see Chapter 7, Tomorrow's Settlements

Tao Paul Wimbush on his smallholding in the Lammas eco-hamlet, Pembrokeshire. Changes in planning law in Wales have made the eco-hamlet possible.

New forms of low-impact settlement are appearing in Wales. See 'The Lammas Project' in Chapter 7, Tomorrow's Settlements

Photovoltaic panels for renewable electricity on a smallholding at Lammas.

Tao Paul and Hoppi Wimbush's smallholding at Lammas is managed on permaculture principles and so is ecologically complex. An important aim is to augment soil fertility.

The UK's rural soils are becoming dangerously infertile: see 'The Agrarian Future' in Chapter 8, Through the Political Miasma

CHAPTER 1
GRINDING GROWTH

INCHING TOWARDS A NEW PURPOSE

Repercussions of the quest for perpetual growth are whacking us about the head and everywhere else.

The combination of finite planet with infinite economic growth and population expansion is a logical impossibility, but that does not stop politicians and business leaders from seeking it. Businesses want to expand their market share, and politicians think they have to offer voters visions of greater affluence achieved through economic growth.

But the faster the rate of expansion, the quicker we reach the limits to growth.

The growth model is broken. We need a new model, and the world is slowly, painfully, assembling a new one. Wales, where I live, is making more progress than many nations, as I hope to show, but even in this land of the Well-being of Future Generations Bill,[1] there are glaring inconsistencies and contradictions to be negotiated.

UNAFFORDABLE LIVING

Take one household, just about able to pay the regular bills for food, heat, light and transport to and from work. To increase consumption the household needs more income or lower taxes, or a mixture of both. Wages, salaries and self-employed income account for the majority, 71%, of gross household income.[2] If wages go up, employers have to find more income from which to pay. If taxes go down, public services have to be axed, so people working in and for the public sector lose their jobs.

The adults in this household may opt to reduce their own consumption. They take low-waged local jobs and live frugally, but

1

the sums still don't add up. They can no longer afford council tax – levied on the value of the family's home, not on their income – and they can't pay their electricity or gas bills, and they fall behind with their mortgage or rent payments. This is painting a black picture, because working adults can still claim tax credits to increase their income, but the criteria for claiming are drawn tighter and tighter. If they can't find jobs, they are already in a very sticky situation because of the benefits cap which came into force across England, Scotland and Wales between April and October 2013. The cap was, in 2014-15, £350 a week for a single person aged 25-59, without children, working fewer than 30 hours a week, and £500 for all other types of household, regardless of the number of children.

The benefits cap prevents many low-to-middle income households from living in London. Checking on the website Rightmove in summer 2014 for the cheapest two-bedroom flat in London E1 – including the 'Jack the Ripper'[3] district of Whitechapel, which until recently was 'affordable' -- I found one at £290 a week. The others were all over £300 a week. Three bedrooms? Just one at £300 a week, all the others, £350 and above.

When the rent of a downmarket two-bedroom flat in east London is between 50% and 60% of the median take-home pay of a private-sector worker in the capital,[4] trouble is not ahead, it has already arrived. The benefits cap is supposed to be equivalent to the average income of working households across the UK, but in the roar-away city of London it bites ferociously. London accounted for about half of the net population increase in the UK in 2013,[5] and is also a 'safe haven' for wealthy investors, who are buying up properties for cash (and quite often leaving them empty).

Chart 1: London leads pay table – but rents are unaffordable for many

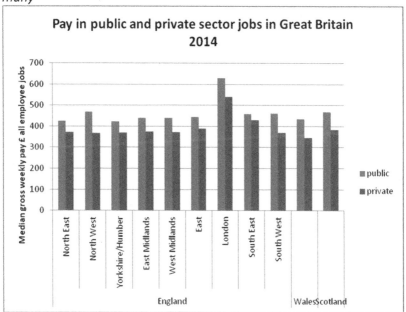

Pay in public and private sector jobs in Great Britain 2014

Source: Office for National Statistics, Annual Survey of Hours and Earnings 2014, provisional table 25.1a

London wages exceed those in other regions by a mile, as Chart 1 shows. The median gross weekly wage in 2014 was £565.40 a week across the public and private sectors, compared with £379.50 in Wales, the lowest-wage part of Great Britain.[6] London is the jobs magnet, alone accounting for 15.6%, almost one in six, of employee jobs in Great Britain, and London and the South East together for 29.6%, nearly three in ten.

Chart 2: Where the jobs are

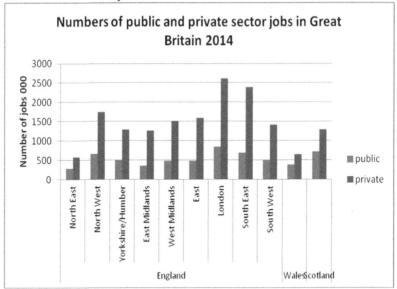

Source: *Office for National Statistics, Annual Survey of Hours and Earnings 2014, provisional table 25.1a*

Rents for two-bedroom flats are cheaper where I live in Wales, from about £80 a week in the town of Carmarthen, but wages are low, too, clustered at and near the minimum wage of £6.31 per hour at age 21-plus, £5.03 for ages 18-20. The overall median wage for Wales is in fact higher than it would be if the proportion of public-sector jobs was more typical of the rest of Great Britain. The public sector paid a median £88 a week more than the private sector in Wales in 2014, and public-sector jobs account for 35% of the total, compared with 20.3% in South East England, where the wage differential was just £28.70.

In Britain today it costs a great deal just to exist in a subsistence way. These costs have led to another problem – massive levels of debt. The average total debt per household in October 2014 was about £54,700.[7]

4

Chart 3: Lending to individuals in the UK – debts accumulating

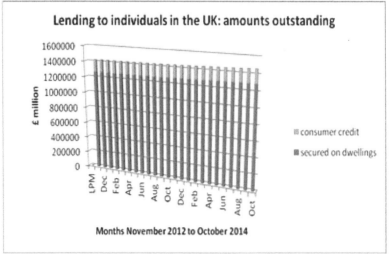

Lending to individuals in the UK: amounts outstanding

£ million

Months November 2012 to October 2014

■ consumer credit

■ secured on dwellings

Source: Bank of England Bank stats for October 2014, from table A5.2, seasonally adjusted. The data excludes student loans. 'LPM' stands for monetary data published monthly.

Families in debt lack the freedom to start living in a radically different way unless they opt for an extreme downshift, selling their home and possessions to repay their debts and starting again outside the modern model of consumer society.

TYPOLOGIES OF GREEN

Green campaigners often concentrate on protests against environmental destruction and climate change, but less often against the networks of power which control the exploitation of resources. The splintering of protest between separate activities, whether fracking, or polluting the seas, or crushing animal and plant species to the point of extinction, or paying poverty wages to garment workers in Asia, makes it harder to see all these as manifestations of the pursuit of profit.

We have organised society so that the health of the Earth ecosystem is subordinate to a belief that humans are in charge, and entitled to seek the maximum economic profit from using up all those resources that are accessible to us. It is a doctrine of the survival of the most rapacious, who seem to believe that if only they have 'enough' economic power, they and their descendants will always be able to buy survival. Yet enough is never enough, and so the Great Grab goes on and on, whilst the disregarded billions face polluted and diminishing water supplies, impoverished soils on the pockets of land left to them, or hand-to-mouth existence in noxious slums.

I need think no further back than my own maternal grandparents. My mother's parents, Albert and Lavinia Warinton, achieved a comfortable retirement thanks to the new post-1945 Welfare State in which they spent their later years. Albert was a baker and confectioner and he and Lavinia also ran a catering service. They had a prominent double-fronted shop in the Thames-side town of Chertsey, of which my main memories are sacks of flour, indulgent cakes and the aroma of baked bread. Mum's older sister Alice married a dairy farmer who was an owner-occupier, a big tick in Lavinia's eyes. Lavinia was not impressed when in 1942 mum chose to marry Lionel, whose family rented a smallholding, I think because she saw the word 'insecure' stamped all over the future, even if Lionel survived the rest of the war. Albert had only to contemplate his own grandfathers to understand the misery of unfettered capitalism. His father's father Thomas, also a baker, died poverty-stricken in the Sevenoaks Union Workhouse in 1900, and his mother's father Solomon Crowhurst lost his farm at Hodsoll Street in Kent between 1861 and 1871, when English farming began to suffer competition, especially from the newly exploited lands of the USA, Canada, Australia and New Zealand.[8]

Albert and Lavinia were 'green' in that they wasted nothing, grew their own fruit, vegetables and flowers, and did not engage in conspicuous consumption. They were conservative.

Nowadays, Greens of all types are commonly regarded as radical, while the term 'conservative' has, I think, changed its emphasis from the One Nation paternalistic doctrine of Benjamin Disraeli – rights and obligations -- to 'protection of private interests', prioritising rights to hold wealth over obligations to redistribute it. This world view pushes Greens to the margins, from which remote hinterlands the loudest voices tend to carry furthest.

Kari McGregor in Australia has analysed four separate categories of Green,[9] not mutually exclusive but forming a continuum: Bright Green, Lite Green, Deep Green and Dark Green. Bright Greens promote technology and greenwash innovations like carbon trading, Lite Greens go for 'ethical consumption', Deep Greens aim to block activities which damage the environment, and Dark Greens are resilience builders, preparing to live in a different world without long supply lines, just-in-time deliveries or much in the way of fossil fuels, in many ways not such a different world from the one in which Albert and Lavinia lived.

Splintered Greens are less effective than collaborating Greens, thinks Kari: "A danger with any movement is its potential to fragment into factions once it reaches a certain size – with the various factions competing instead of collaborating – and the potential emergence of a dominant faction that drowns out competing worldviews, theories of change, and tactics," she wrote. "Through this tangled web of worldview, theory and practice there is a need to locate strands of commonalities that can be woven together..."[10]

Good sense, but so far none of these variants of green gives enough importance to developing an economic system which is subsidiary to the planet, rather than seeking to dominate it. The New Economics Foundation,[11] slogan 'economics as if the people and the planet mattered', has moved into this territory, and offers a resource for Deep Greens and Dark Greens to broaden the scope of their ambitions.

I have a long way to go myself, a mottled, weak green splashed with other colours. My 'ecological footprint', courtesy of the Centre for Sustainable Economy,[12] showed that I use resources from 2.16 planets. A similar calculator from WWF (the World Wide Fund for Nature)[13] gave a bigger footprint, 2.28 planets, and if I should fly anywhere again, that figure would soar. To cut down to one planet would mean moving to a smaller home, becoming a vegan and abandoning the car. The vegan issue is complex, because the farms in this hilly part of Wales depend on livestock. The slopes are steep, the soils poor, and farms cannot diversify quickly. Buying local food means buying what is produced locally, and in the case of sheep, that is probably not ideal for the future of the planet. It would be entirely possible to go without a car, provided I did not work, or ever need to visit a doctor or dentist, or shop, because my home village is ten miles from the nearest small town, and the bus service is sparse. I could move to a smaller house, but I am not the only person who has to decide, there is a surfeit of unsold property in the village now that the school has closed, and I love the garden. Cutting back to one planet's worth of resources when world population is growing by 1.1% a year is a double challenge. It took 125 years from 1804 to 1927 for the population to double from 1 billion to 2 billion, but only 13 years, between 1999 and 2012, for 6 billion to become 7 billion.[14] On the Worldometer website[15] the numbers on the births dial fly past almost two and a half times faster than on the deaths dial. Adapting to one planet's resources, when people are multiplying and there is less and less for each individual, means adopting lifestyles that are beyond frugal.

---

[1] The Well-being of Future Generations Bill was progressing through the Welsh Government at the time of writing in 2014. The Bill "strengthens existing governance arrangements for improving the well-being of Wales in order to ensure that the needs of the present are met without compromising the ability of future generations to meet their own needs".

[2] Table 14, average incomes, taxes and benefits by decile groups of all households 2012-13, in personal income and wealth tables, Office for National Statistics.

[3] 'Jack the Ripper' was an unidentified serial murderer in Whitechapel, London, who is believed to have killed at least five women in 1888, and possibly more.

[4] *Annual Survey of Hours and Earnings 2014*, provisional, Office for National Statistics, table 25.1a, all employees by region, public and private sectors. The median gross weekly pay for private-sector jobs in London was £541.60 (but 40% of private-sector jobs paid less than £452.50 a week).

[5] The population of London rose by 108,000 in 2013. See 'London's population is booming, so what's the solution?' by Feargus O'Sullivan, www.theguardian.com/commentisfree/2014/jun/27/london-population-booming-new-york-tokyo, June 27th 2014.

[6] *Annual Survey of Hours and Earnings 2014*, provisional, op.cit. table 25.1a, gross weekly pay for all employee jobs by region.

[7] Estimated number of households in October 2014 26.691 million, based on 2011 Census and population growth from then until autumn 2014.

[8] 'The great depression and recovery, 1874-1914', chapter 18 in Lord Ernle's classic *English Farming Past and Present*, first published by Longman's Green & Co in 1927. The chapter starts: "Since 1862 the tide of agricultural prosperity had ceased to flow; after 1874 it turned, and rapidly ebbed. A period of depression began which, with some fluctuations in severity, continued throughout the rest of the reign of Queen Victoria, and beyond".

[9] 'The spectrum of a movement' by Karl McGregor, www.generationalpha.org/shades-of-green/, October 8th 2014.

[10] www.generationalpha.org/shades-of-green/, as above.

[11] www.neweconomics.org/

[12] www.myfootprint.org/

[13] http://footprint.wwf.org.uk/?homepage&_ga=1.64760047.1787057741.1413827342

[14] World Population Prospects from the United Nations.

[15] www.worldometers.info/

CHAPTER 2
GLOBALISATION: THE POWER TO COLONISE

PRIVATE JETS AND PUBLIC PITTANCES

Finance is global. Trade is global. The impacts are felt by everyone, but what has globalisation done for us? Globalisation has damaged our planet, its climate and ecology. Powerful corporations have used globalisation to grab resources when and where they can. They have built a vast, destructive global weapons industry that coalesces with governments. Governments try to prevent free movement of people while allowing capital to flow wherever the moneyed elite want it to go.

Meanwhile, relatively little official effort has been devoted to reducing, reusing and recycling materials, to researching and developing renewable energies and materials, to limiting urbanisation and to encouraging self-sustaining communities which communicate and collaborate across hundreds and thousands of miles.

David Rothkopf's book *Superclass: the Global Power Elite and the World they are Making,*[1] has a chapter called 'Each one is one in a million', which starts in a Gulfstream Aerospace factory in Georgia, USA. A private Gulfstream jet is a badge of the global elite, their means of intercontinental travel. While the passengers of commercial airlines shuffle through security checks, displaying their apparel and hand luggage to sundry security personnel, surveillance cameras, scanners and sniffer dogs, in a humiliating if precautionary process of spot-the-terrorist, Gulfstream owners and their associates are lords of the skies. Rothkopf writes[2] that private jet passengers "do not wait in lines. They are not buffeted by rude airline personnel or security staff, or delayed by an unending stream of circumstances beyond their control. Bags are whisked to aircraft. Arrival arrangements are made by concierges. And in moments, without passing through security, with less fuss than it takes to enter a typical office building today, they are airborne on flights whose routes they determine, whose menus are catered to their needs and wants".

Gulfstream is part of the US defence company General Dynamics and thus intimately connected with the world arms business. Globalised arms sales are a terrifying outcome of our competitive history, our struggle to survive the dangers of living on an unstable planet alongside other life forms that can weaken us, poison us, injure us or kill us. Carlo M Cipolla, in his 1962 book *The Economic History of World Population*, wrote[3] that in his opinion "[f]or more than nine-tenths of its existence, the entire human race has lived in a state of complete savagery". This legacy of "the most cruel selective process" created man as a particularly aggressive creature, said Cipolla, who ended his book pleading for quality of life and of judgement to be prioritised above numbers of people and possessions: "What man today desperately needs is the kind of education that allows him to make a wise use of the techniques he possesses", so that we can overcome the failing of Philippe II, Duke of Orléans, Regent during the minority of Louis XV of France, who according to Cipolla "had all the talents except the talent to make use of them".

Critical thinking is not particularly encouraged in our examination-dominated schools, where the main business is to attach as many certificates as possible to each student. Certificates, except at elite levels, are awarded for knowing stuff, rarely for questioning the validity or merits of the stuff itself. Education has become a branch of the economy, a form of consumer purchase, sold as a gateway into the global economy.

Yet globalisation has created a new world order in which the wealthiest 1%, 72.30 million persons, claim ownership of wealth worth some $110 trillion, equivalent to the wealth of the poorest half of the population, amounting to more than 3.61 billion people.[4] Even more starkly, Oxfam calculated that just 85 individuals own wealth of $1.7 trillion, averaging $20 billion each.[5] In contrast, about 3 billion cannot accumulate much wealth because their annual income totals less than $1000 – that's under £594.[6] Try living in Western Europe or North America on less than £600 a year.

Globalisation was sold to the public as the path to efficient economics, each country majoring on its natural advantages. The plan might have worked better if nations were also self-contained economic units, but the economic power lies in corporations, who use it for their own benefit.

BILLIONS OF MILES, BILLIONS OF POUNDS

Private jet owners will probably secure enough fuel to keep themselves airborne even when mass long-haul tourism is on the wane, damaged by costlier fuel or its counterpart, smaller incomes, and by rising social instability underneath flight paths and in popular destinations. But what sort of world will they be circling over?

The frantic rush to exploit fossil fuel resources with a low return on energy invested in extraction is proof that easier, cheaper sources have gone. Competition for what is left is neither gentlemanly nor fair.

When alcohol was prohibited in the USA between 1920 and 1933, gangsters who cornered illegal supplies made a great deal of money, if they survived the vicious battles for control of the lucrative but outlawed business. The big differences between alcohol and oil include the fact that alcohol was cheap to produce and there was scant risk of world supplies diminishing to a trickle. When the end of cheap fossil oil is looming – because the costs of extraction will be greater than consumers can afford -- the battles to control the sources of the most cheaply drilled oil are likely to be fiercer than the struggles to corner alcohol supplies.

Peaceable small farmers aren't going to be at the head of the queue for oil, although modern food production, processing and distribution is based upon the plentiful supply of cheap oil and gas, enabling a very few people to feed everyone else.

In the UK, more than 99% of the population are neither farmers nor their spouses, nor farm workers, nor farm business directors. What are they all going to eat when energy shortages kick in and the costs of transporting meat and fish, fruit and vegetables, cereals and milk, across the globe become prohibitive? They will have to find their food closer to home, at a time when farmers will be trying to cope with shifting climate zones, unpredictable weather, and the prospects of instability in the supply and costs of seeds, fertilisers, pesticides and fuel.

'Food miles', the distances travelled by foodstuffs from farm to plate, are often colossal. They have been justified on the alleged basis of providing markets for small farmers, and choice for consumers in affluent countries. In reality, small farmers are often ousted by corporations, and public demand for choice is augmented hugely by advertising.

Arrival in the destination country is only a staging point. In the UK, for example, each year about 333 million tonnes of foods are transported across the nation, generating 415 billion tonne-kilometres of transport (mainly on roads).[7]

It's wasteful, polluting, and the outcome of corporations' global expansionism, which has been assisted hugely by free trade policies. Global food flows allowed supermarket companies to develop until they controlled food retailing, but supermarkets no longer have everything their own way. Local foods are increasingly popular here in the UK, leading to a modest revival in specialist food shops and providing markets for producers of top quality and out-of-the-ordinary foodstuffs. In 2014 Transition Tywi Trawsnewid in Carmarthenshire, one of the rising number of Transition Town groups, worked with The Green House shop in Llandeilo – a shop which raises money for environmental causes – to produce a local food guide, and it soon became clear that a bigger version would be required for 2015. Interest in local food, and in growing your own food, is on the up, while supermarkets have lost their novelty appeal and in 2014 Tesco, Sainsbury's and Morrisons all reported falling sales.

FREE TRADE: A BOON FOR CORPORATIONS

No population can survive without food, therefore it is a strong argument that governments should prioritise secure food supplies.

Free-trade food policies are based on the belief that food should come from areas of the world that can produce it at the lowest immediate cost. Detrimentally for our future, the lowest immediate cost takes no account of environmental degradation, or fossil energy or water depletion, or the livelihoods of small-scale farmers who are affected by globalised food chains.

The protagonists for free trade generally claim that tariff barriers and financial support schemes which protect farmers in the affluent world mean that farmers in 'developing' countries cannot compete successfully, despite their lower labour costs. Yet small-scale farmers in Africa, Latin America and Asia are the last to benefit from free trade. The cash benefits go to large farmers and corporations, for planting crops for export[8] rather than food crops for local consumption.

The World Trade Organization (WTO), which pursues the free trade objectives of industrial nations and multinational corporations, is aiming for open trade flows all around the globe. The 'Doha[9] Round' of WTO negotiations began in November 2001, and had not been concluded as this was written in 2015.

Major corporations exert huge influence on the WTO because of their scale. The Western world's three largest companies are Wal-Mart Stores, Shell, and ExxonMobil. Wal-Mart Stores' annual sales, $476.3 billion in the year to January 31st 2014, are similar to the gross domestic product (GDP) of Taiwan, which according to the International Monetary Fund (IMF) was the world's 25th largest national economy in 2013. Shell's 2013 sales of $451.2 billion, and Exxon Mobil's sales in 2013, $438.3 billion, exceed the GDP of Austria, the country ranked 27th by GDP in the IMF's ranking.

Free trade clears the way for international companies to expand their activities across the globe, to create transport networks across thousands of miles and many national borders, to build tariff-free supply chains. Corporations are driven by the imperative to make money. They do not have to offer welfare to the population, and they rely (usually) on the armed forces of nation states to defend them. Corporations have the luxury of single-minded pursuit of their objectives.

Finding hard data on transnational corporations' share of world trade is complicated. Perhaps the data is scarce because it is not in corporations' interests to highlight the extent of their private trade flows, but whatever the reason, accurate information for the public is limited. The 'shadow' website www.gatt.org, which sharply criticises the WTO, estimated[10] in 2010 that just the 200 largest multinationals accounted for 28% of global trade. In corporations' eyes, that was nowhere near enough. They want to grow, grow, grow, but the Doha Round talks dragged on and on, and they became impatient. Talks on three huge new neoliberal trade agreements are under way, as far below public consciousness as possible. They would embody staggering concessions to corporations, in the form of investment treaties enabling corporations to sue governments for policy changes detrimental to corporate interests.

The first of the Super Three is the **Trans-Pacific Partnership (TPP)**, between the USA, Canada, Mexico, Peru, Chile, Australia, New Zealand, Japan, Singapore, Vietnam, Brunei and Malaysia. Talks, which began in 2008, explore means of opening intellectual property and public services to open competition.

Secondly, the **Trade in Services Agreement (TISA)**, involving the EU and 20 other countries, came on the horizon in 2012. TISA would cover health, education, energy, water and drainage services, construction, finance, banking, insurance, transport and retailing, opening them all up to corporate competition. Such a deal would mean the end of public control of the UK's National Health Service, because corporations would be able to sue governments for policy changes they disliked.

Summer 2013 saw the launch of talks between the EU and the USA on a **Transatlantic Trade and Investment Partnership (TTIP)**. The theme is competition right across the economy, including health and education, with corporations empowered to challenge prudent regulations -- including regulation of finance -- as barriers to trade.

Just why governments are so keen to hand power over to corporations is hard to fathom, unless politicians feel they are all on the same side – the side of private exploitation. Policy changes to which corporations objected would be impossible, unless the offending government paid compensation at full 'market' value plus compound interest. In countries where corporations are in dominant control, people are regarded as completely disposable factors of production. Take Guatemala.

THE DISTRESS OF GUATEMALA

Guatemala in Central America is a stunning country both for its peoples and landscapes and for the corruption of its governments down the years. The indigenous peoples continue to suffer from domination by a tiny number of foreign corporations and their local enforcers.

I spent six weeks in Guatemala in autumn 2007, staying with a family and helping out at a UK-funded school, Escuela Proyecto La Esperanza, in Jocotenango. On Friday October 12th 2007 I was part of a small group travelling to the Mayan ruins at Tikal, in the forests of the Petén. We had to cross Guatemala City, which I remember for ubiquitous McDonalds; Esso, Shell and Texaco filling stations; and high-rise American hotels, encircled by tin-roofed shacks, unfriendly streets, potholes, rubbish and guns.

We followed the CA9 highway north-east out of Guatemala City to El Progreso, Rio Hondo and Quirigua, where there are intricate Maya carvings. Quirigua is in the Motagua river valley, which reaches the Caribbean at Puerto Barrios, Guatemala's only significant port on the Caribbean.

Most of the valley land is owned by corporations, with fruit plantations and horticultural crops for export, the latter protected by acre upon acre of plastic. The bananas are plastic-protected too, encased in perforated blue plastic to protect against rain, dust and wind. Insecticides were not mentioned, but on plantations which are not 'organic' it is usual for bags to be impregnated with insecticide. What a lot of plastic to replace when the oil runs out, because most plastics are derived from oil. At Quirigua the plantations belong to Chiquita Brands --descendent of the infamous United Fruit Company -- and to Del Monte.

North from the Motagua valley through the Petén to the ruined Maya city of Tikal, we passed a succession of shiny new evangelical protestant churches (financed from the USA), set in decrepit villages. The farms visible from the road were either under two hectares or vast, containing much unused land. Most of the land north of the little town of Frontera, where the Lago de Izabal narrows into the Caribbean-bound Rio Dulce, is controlled by a handful of powerful families. They used to run cattle, tended by local labourers, but since the road was hard-surfaced in the years around 2000, the labourers have migrated away, to the slums of Guatemala City and as illegals to the USA.

Staying overnight in Finca Ixobel, a country guesthouse owned by an American widow whose Guatemalteco husband was assassinated by a death squad in the 'civil war' between 1960 and 1996, in which some 200,000 people died or 'disappeared', I read in *Revue* magazine for June 2007 that over a fifth of the population, 21%, have to exist on less than $1 (59p) a day, and well over half the people, 58%, subsist on less than $2 (£1.18) a day.

The Petén is, according to Tikal guide Pablo, the world's fifth largest forest reserve, and the biggest in Central America. The reserve also functions as a drugs highway. Drug runners are constantly building air strips deep in the forest for the lucrative *narcotrafico*, which finances grand villas behind high walls, and four-by-fours with tinted windows. Drugs are more important to the local economy than tourism, despite the presence of amazing Mayan monuments. "Each year around 150,000 visitors come to Tikal," said Pablo. Increasingly, they fly in to nearby Flores Airport, to avoid the hazards to life and limb in Guatemala City. Flores Airport has brought 'development' to the Petén, shopping malls plonked incongruously in the rural landscape. Pablo was pessimistic. He said that poverty was increasing because subsistence farmers did not have enough land. The landlords opposed any process of land reform, even though their own land might lie idle. They were looking forward to a golden era of biofuels, a scenario in which small farmers, *campesinos,* do not feature. Fewer families could now afford to send their children to school, and in Pablo's view the illiteracy rate was escalating again, above the low point of 40% estimated in 2002.

In Guatemala the law of the jugular applies. There are courts, and prisons, but legal procedures are slow and uncertain, and extra-judicial killings commonplace.

The apparatus of the state in Guatemala, such as exists, is deployed to protect existing power structures. The welfare of the people comes way down this agenda: politicians and businessmen – the same people, often at the same times – have little interest in working to abolish hunger among the indigenous peoples, to provide affordable healthcare, or to create a thriving countryside where families can produce enough food for themselves and their neighbourhoods.

The indigenous Maya people believed that man was merely part of the natural order on Earth, a natural order that needed to remain in balance. When their practice departed calamitously from this tidy theory, their civilisation declined. Over a thousand years ago, the results of Mayan culture's linkage of religion with astronomy was causing catastrophe, as huge, astronomically-aligned temples and monuments, in socially and occupationally complex cities, absorbed too much of the people's collective energy, and demanded too much food, fuel and construction materials from the rural hinterlands. The forest was felled.

As resources dwindled, Mayan tribes fought intense wars to try and seize as much as they could of the remaining food and water. The knock-out blow at Tikal was a 30-year drought around 1000AD. The occupants of Tikal walked away, and many of their descendants – still poverty-stricken -- live in the western highlands of Guatemala, on steep, infertile land which the European families and the multinational corporations have not wanted.

The relationship between trees and human survival is too often overlooked, ignored. Jared Diamond, in *Collapse: How Societies Choose to Fail or Survive*[11] points out that forests

> "....function as the world's major air filter removing carbon monoxide and other air pollutants, and forests and their soils are a major sink for carbon, with the result that deforestation is an important driving force behind global warming by decreasing that carbon sink. Water transpiration from trees returns water to the atmosphere, so that deforestation tends to cause diminished rainfall and increased desertification. Trees retain water in the soil and keep it moist. They protect the land surface against landslides, erosion, and sediment runoff into streams. Some forests, notably tropical rainforests, hold the major portion of an ecosystem's nutrients, so that logging and carting the logs away tends to leave the cleared land infertile."
>
> -- *Collapse: How Societies Choose to Fail or Survive*, p.469 in 2006 Penguin edition

This is what happened at Tikal and in exploited lands all over the world, from Norse Greenland to Haiti in the Caribbean, from Easter Island in the Pacific to Rwanda in Africa. Deforestation ends societies, even civilisations.

Once free of human interference, the jungle returned to Tikal and clothed the monuments, which slept undisturbed for centuries, while the Mayans were conquered and later dragged unwillingly into a capitalist economy.

Mayans are relatively indifferent to consumer culture, a 'failing' which annoys foreign entrepreneurs:

> "An enormous disadvantage for this country is that the Indians *[the Mayans]* won't work more than just enough to fill their basic needs, and these are very few. The only way to make *[a Mayan]* work is to advance him money, then he can be forced to work. Very often, they run off, but they are caught and punished very severely."
>
> -- from the story of a German who emigrated to Guatemala in 1892, told in Daniel Wilkinson's *Silence on the Mountain: Stories of Terror, Betrayal and Forgetting in Guatemala*, p.38.[12]

This German immigrant, Friedrich Endler, ran a coffee plantation. The plantations struggled to find enough labour, so the government instituted a form of slavery, the labour draft. Daniel Wilkinson explains this system in *Silence on the Mountain,* a moving and tragic analysis of Guatemala in the 20[tth] century:

> "The labor drafts. Upon the request of a plantation owner, the governors of each department would round up a work gang of fifty to one hundred Indians and send them to work on the plantation. An 1894 law provided Indians with one way to escape this form of forced recruitment: become an indebted worker for a plantation."
>
> -- *Silence on the Mountain* p.76-77

The pass laws, so hated in South Africa later in the 20th century, already existed in Guatemala:

> " 'We were slaves because of the law of Ubico,' recalled the next elderly peasant we talked to. He was referring to President Jorge Ubico, who had governed the country from 1930 to 1944, and the 'slavery' he described was not debt peonage but the vagrancy laws that had replaced it. 'We had to carry a booklet, like an identity card, which showed what plantation we worked in and how many hours we had worked that year. If you didn't carry it, the government could jail you and make you work without pay'."
>
> -- *Silence on the Mountain* p.97

Land is at the heart of the unhappy history of Guatemala. Immigrants with access to capital claimed it. Government was for them, not for the Mayans, and there was no question of prioritising rights for the indigenous peoples above rights for plantation owners to obtain as much profit as possible. The landowners have benefited financially from colonisation and its successor, free trade, because they have deliberately marginalised the indigenous peoples.

FEEDING ASIA FROM SOUTH AMERICA

Back in 2005, Alberto Weisser, chief executive officer of the agribusiness company Bunge, the world's largest processor of oilseeds, spoke to an AgriVision conference in the Netherlands.[13] He said:

> "It is estimated that nearly 600 million people in the Asia-Pacific region – significantly more than the entire population of the European Union – will move from rural areas to cities by 2020. That is 600 million people that *(sic)* will be buying food rather than growing it."

Bunge, headquartered in St Louis, Missouri, intended to supply a lot of the food that would be required. Where would it come from? Alberto Weisser appeared to rule out China because of water shortages, but probably also because of geopolitical realities: foreign corporations cannot yet walk into China and take over huge tracts of land on which to develop an industrial style of farming.[14] One huge country which has welcomed foreign buyers is Brazil, the country containing the world's largest remaining expanse of rain forest. Bunge wanted to grow more soya beans in Brazil, for export to Asia. By 2014, said Weisser, South America would provide 75% of global soya exports.

Did this happen? In 2013 half of global soya exports came from South America, grain traders Nidera reported.[15] Not 75%, but still a colossal contribution. In something of a rearguard action against overseas buyers, mega-exporters Argentina and Brazil have laws to restrict foreign ownership. Argentina's 2011 *ley de tierras* says that no single foreign entity can own more than 1,000 hectares or more than 15% of land in any state or municipality. Brazil had passed a similar law in 1971 which was rarely enforced, but it was revived in

2010 when the retiring Brazilian president Luiz Inacio Lula da Silva approved the introduction of new limits on foreign ownership of Brazilian land, to a maximum of 5,000 hectares, with no single holding to exceed 25% of the area of the municipality where it is located.[16] Yet within a year, by spring 2011, Lula da Silva's successor as president, Dilma Rousseff, headed a government that appeared less sure about controlling foreign investment. The agriculture minister, Wagner Rossi, pledged a relaxation of the law restricting foreign land holdings, to attract more investment from agribusiness corporations.[17] If Brazil, the world's seventh largest economy,[18] feels the need to open its farmland to global corporations, surely smaller and poorer countries have even less capacity to resist.

Bunge's Alberto Weisser was in 2005 calling for a "significant expansion of existing logistics systems" (i.e. roads and port terminals) necessary for Brazilian soya production to soar further:

> "In an average harvest season, truck line-ups for unloading at public facilities in Paranagua [19] can stretch for 100 kilometres....We estimate that inefficiency in the ports led to over $1 billion in demurrage[20] costs last year."

A line of trucks stretching, hours and days at a time, for 100 kilometres – nearly 63 miles – was already carrying an awful lot of food out of Brazil.

The rain forests in the Amazon basin, rich in species, where the indigenous peoples have knowledge of the nutritional and medicinal value of plants, knowledge amassed over millennia, are cut down. Cattle are shifted northwards from their grazing lands into the clearings, and their former grazing grounds are cultivated for soya and other export crops. The rain forest would be vanishing at an even faster rate if Brazil had better roads. Companies including Bunge are helping to fund them. The 1,100-mile Cuiabá to Santarém highway, from the Mato Grosso in central Brazil northwards to the port of Santarém, where the Tapajós river flows into the Amazon, 'opens up' the Amazon rainforest to development. The land made accessible by the road receives doses of synthetic fertilisers to boost (for a short time) its capacity to grow food crops and biomass for fuel, but the ecological diversity of the forest disappears.

Bunge is big, with annual sales of $61.3 billion in 2013, but not the largest conglomerate with deep involvement in Brazilian agribusiness. Others include

- Cargill, based in Minneapolis, Minnesota, a huge private company which does not put a great deal of information into the public domain. Cargill, 90% owned by the Cargill family, recorded revenues of $136.7 billion in 2013.
- Archer Daniels Midland Company, of Decatur, Illinois, 2013 sales $89.8 billion.
- André Maggi Group of Brazil.

The André Maggi Group is headed by Blairo Maggi, ex-governor of the Brazilian state of Mato Grosso and by 2014 a dollar billionaire, as were his mother Lucia, sister Marli and brother-in-law Itamar Locks.

"The future," said Bunge's Alberto Weisser in 2005, "will be one of an ever more sophisticated, seamless production chain." That process has accelerated, and would be given further impetus by the trade agreements which so many governments seem eager to sign, and against which national land laws would soon be tested.

Meanwhile, governments and corporate bodies in food-poor countries scour the world for land. The database landmatrix.org records nearly 2,000 major deals since 2000. They include China securing farmland all over the globe, including separate contracts for 100,000 hectares in Zimbabwe, 200,000 in the Philippines and almost 240,000 in Papua New Guinea. Saudi Arabia's deals include 200,000 hectares in the Philippines, too. Dry Qatar has the output from over 101,000 hectares in sub-Saharan Sudan. Malaysia has a huge 470,000-hectare land contract in the Democratic Republic of Congo, which is attracting foreign investors in land as well as minerals, despite a volatile and corrupt political context.

Farming as an Extractive Industry

The globalisation of agriculture, following in the wake of its industrialisation, has been catastrophically wasteful. Industrial agriculture uses, per acre, between six and ten times more energy than traditional farming.

Agriculture is responsible for about a quarter of Earth's carbon dioxide emissions, for 60% of methane, and 80% of nitrous oxide.[21] These three gases are the leading contributors to man-made climate change.[22] Agriculture's share of global water consumption is nearly 70%, and farms use more and more pumped irrigation water to counteract soil drying after prolonged exposure to sunlight. Water extracted for irrigation is causing groundwater levels to fall. The production of export crops on a large scale, on the same land year after year, exhausts the soil and local biosystems. Manufactured fertilisers, particularly nitrogen, give yields a short-term boost, acting rather like sugar in humans. Natural gas is a major feedstock for sugar-aping nitrogen fertilisers.

Industrial agriculture would not be possible without powered farm machinery. Ground cover plants preserve soil moisture and soil carbon content, and trees add to the protective canopy, but machines work most efficiently in large fields, without trees or hedges, the type of field that is vulnerable to soil drying and erosion.

Industrial agriculture in a world of global free trade does not help populations in poor countries to feed themselves. Quite the opposite: between 50% and 80% of farmland in low-income nations is used to provide agricultural commodities for export – a point reinforced by Bunge's strategy to use Brazil as the food bowl for the distant Asia Pacific region.

Globalisation for profit has given a few hundred million people, who happened to be born in particular places at specific times, material standards of consumption so high that they are living in bubbles, insulated from the damage that resource exploitation inflicts on the majority of humankind, and on the Earth. Living in the most luxurious bubbles of billionaires' private islands, palatial houses, bullet-proof cars and Gulfstream jets tends to be conveyed in the media as a reward for being exceptionally talented, a lifestyle to which, in the 'equality of opportunity' agenda, everyone can aspire. Perhaps it is an inevitable consequence of a culture dominated by the economy that oodles of money should be seen as the ultimate success symbol, but the mass pursuit of that goal is like the Medieval dream of turning base metal into gold. It cannot be done.

---

[1] *Superclass: the Global Power Elite and the World they are Making*, by David Rothkopf, published in the USA in 2008 by Farrar, Straus and Giroux and in the UK also in 2008 by Little, Brown.

[2] Rothkopf, op.cit. p.28.

[3] *The Economic History of World Population*, by Carlo M Cipolla, 1964 Penguin edition, p.112. First published 1962.

[4] Population on May 13th 2014 from www.geohive.com.

[5] *Working for the Few: Political capture and economic inequality*, Oxfam Briefing Paper 178 by Ricardo Fuentes-Nieva and Nicholas Galasso. Summary, January 20th 2014.

[6] www.globalissues.org/article/26/poverty-facts-and-stats, accessed May 13th 2014.

[7] BioEthics Education Project, www.beep.ac.uk, accessed May 13th 2014.

[8] The areas used for export crops grown in poor countries are often called 'ghost acres'. For every agricultural acre within the UK, there are at least two overseas, producing food for British consumers. See 'Measuring food by the mile' by Tim Lobstein, www.mcspotlight.org/media/reports/foodmiles.html , based on data gathered in 1993 and 1994.

[9] Doha is in Qatar.

[10] www.gatt.org/trastat_e.html, accessed on November 6th 2010.

[11] London and New York: Allen Lane and Viking Penguin, 2005.

[12] *Silence on the Mountain* by Daniel Wilkinson was published in 2004 by Duke University Press.

[13] Formerly available at www.bunge.com/US/en/media/AgrivisionsSpeechWeb.pdf

[14] Foreign investors can acquire rights to use state-owned urban land for specific periods of time, but not rural land: see 'What are the legal issues associated with foreign ownership of land in China?' www.terralex.org/publication/f166f4f8ee, accessed on November 6th 2010.

[15] Quoted on *Farmers Weekly Interactive*, www.fwi.co.uk/articles/16/01/2014/142792/south-america-could-hold-key-to-crop-forecasts.htm, January 16th 2014.

[16] 'Brazil – limiting foreign land ownership' in *Meat Trade News Daily*, www.meattradenewsdaily.co.uk/news/060910/brazil___limiting_foreign_land_ow nership_.aspx, September 19th 2010.

[17] 'Brazil in quest to seize farming opportunity' by Joe Leahy, www.ft.com/cms/s/0/01d622fc-481b-11e0-b323-00144feab49a.html#axzz3EvA8X1fD, March 6th 2011.

[18] According to the International Monetary Fund.

[19] Paranagua is the seaport for the city of Curitiba, the capital of Paraná state, and lies between Rio de Janeiro to the north and Porto Alegre to the south.

[20] Demurrage is a charge payable to a ship owner to recompense for failure to load or unload the ship within the agreed time frame.

[21] The figures in this paragraph are from 'How to feed people under a regime of climate change' by Edward Goldsmith, *World Affairs Journal* Vol.7 No.3 July-September 2003, www.edwardgoldsmith.org/32/how-to-feed-people-under-a-regime-of-climate-change/. *World Affairs Journal* is published in India: D-322 Defence Colony, New Delhi 110024, India.

[22] 'Nitrous oxide emissions could double by 2050, study finds' by Robert McSweeney, October 28th 2014, www.carbonbrief.org/blog/2014/10/nitrous-oxide-emissions-could-double-by-2050-study-finds/

CHAPTER 3
HANGING ON BY OUR FINGERNAILS

CLIMATE CHANGE VERSUS GROWTH CONUNDRUM

'Climate' is a fluid concept. The Earth's climates have altered many times in the past, when human meddling was not a factor. The Pleistocene, the seventh major Ice Age that geologists have recorded, started perhaps some 1.8 million years ago in what is now Europe, although scientific opinions differ and the cooling may have begun much earlier. About 73,500 years ago, during the Pleistocene, a super-volcanic eruption in the Lake Toba region of the Indonesian island of Sumatra triggered severe further cooling.[1] The vast clouds of gases and ash emitted from the volcano included sulphur dioxide which was converted to sulphuric acid in the upper atmosphere. This formed a barrier between Earth and the sun's energy, sending the heat back away from Earth. The eruption may have cooled the Earth by 3 to 5 degrees C, a cataclysmic event resulting in species extinctions and probably a drastic reduction in the numbers of humans. Some would have died from suffocation by ash and gases, but even more serious was the long-lasting catastrophic impact on food sources.

The ecological recovery from the Toba eruption was probably slow because of the cold climate over much of the world. The Pleistocene itself ended 10,000 to 12,000 years ago, at the dawn of our historical memory when some humans lived in settled communities, and no longer spent their time as nomadic hunter gatherers. As the ice sheets receded, new lands appeared and humans colonised them.

Any significant climate alteration, no matter how it is caused, can threaten the viability of life as we know it. The strands of natural and human-generated climate change are exceedingly complicated to unravel, but over the span of geological time, natural changes have been colossal and, in our terms, both catastrophic and unstoppable.

Although scientists' warnings about climate change become more strident year by year, too many politicians continue to bury the issues as deeply as they dare.

Back in 2006, the World Bank[2] issued warnings about the impact of natural disasters, both climatic and geological:

"The impact of natural disasters on economic well-being and human suffering has increased alarmingly. In the past year alone, the earthquake and tsunami in the Indian Ocean killed an estimated 200,000 people and left 1.5 million people homeless, catastrophic flooding and mudslides in Guatemala killed hundreds of people, and a massive earthquake in Kashmir killed tens of thousands more in Pakistan and India.

"The death tolls are staggering, and the costs to the human and economic development of the affected countries are huge and rising. Natural disasters are becoming more costly: in constant dollars, disaster costs between 1990 and 1999 were more than 15 times higher ($652 billion in material losses) than they were between 1950 and 1959 ($38 billion at 1998 values). The human cost is also high: over the 1984-2003 period, more than 4.1 billion people were affected by natural disasters. The number affected has grown, from 1.6 billion in the first half of that period (1984-93) to almost 2.6 billion in the second half (1994-2003), and has continued to increase."

Four years later, in 2010, the World Bank and the United Nations jointly published *Natural Hazards, UnNatural Disasters: the Economics of Effective Prevention*. The report overview makes strange reading, because it assumes that economic growth will continue. The World Bank did acknowledge the threat of climate change, but ignored other hazards such as diminishing fossil fuel supplies, environmental destruction and acute financial instability. The report looked at dangers that are already present, such as monsoon and hurricane flooding, and assumed that the resources to cope will be available. The introductory release on the report quotes task team leader Apurva Sanghi as saying:

> "Growing cities will expose more people and property to hazards, but growing cities also suggest growing incomes, which means people are better able to adapt. A rise in vulnerability is not inevitable, if cities are well run."

The messages are that cities will be larger but wealthier, and that wealth enables people to buy security. The report does not indicate where the new wealth is to come from, but it does offer several "common sense" measures, including better weather forecasting; provision of land titles to individuals, who would thus be encouraged to invest in safer structures; removal of rent controls to give landlords incentives to maintain buildings; and reorientation of public spending on maintenance tasks such as mending potholes, painting bridges and cleaning drains.

In essence the report calls for more financial transfers from the public to private sectors. It has some useful ideas for limiting the impact of disasters in the context of oil-rich civilisation. After all, who would argue against better weather forecasting, or cleaner drains? These responses are nowhere near adequate enough, though, to mitigate future disasters in a crowded, polluted, and thirsty world.

In the UK, Sir Nicholas Stern co-ordinated a review for the Treasury on the impact of climate change. The review,[3] published in 2006, poses questions which cannot really be answered because the ecology of the biosphere changes in unpredictable ways. Any system can display "behaviour that is unpredictable from an observation of the interactions of its component parts"[4] because interactions between system components can create hitherto non-existent emergent properties.

Trying to reduce the complexity of climate change to costs in familiar dollars or pounds, as Sir Nicholas was tasked to do, creates an illusion of control, on the lines of 'if we can measure the impacts, then surely we are half way to overcoming them...'. But we cannot measure what is impossible to forecast.

Jonathan Sinclair Wilson, former managing director of the publishers Earthscan, made some fundamental points in his written evidence[5] to the Stern Review:

"Climate scientists have proposed various 'safe' levels of concentration [of CO_2] that will restrict potential temperature rises to no more than 2ºC – at 550ppm,[6] 500ppm or even a mere 430ppm – but as the whole biosphere is involved, in truth very little is known about the interrelated and cumulative feedback processes that may be triggered at particular levels and temperatures.

"In fact, if the most recent annual increases in CO_2 concentrations represent a trend, the rate of increase is accelerating, which itself could be an early sign of positive feedback mechanisms reinforcing the warming process.

"This surely raises the question of whether economic models are able to capture the significance of climatic changes, if those [changes] set limits or constitute threats to the conditions for our collective survival."

Scientists at the UK Meteorological Office's 'Avoiding Dangerous Climate Change' conference in Exeter in 2005 heard from Dr Malte Meinshausen, then of the Swiss Federal Institute of Technology,[7] that an atmospheric concentration of 400 ppm (parts per million) of carbon dioxide equivalent would be a probable danger threshold. The measure 'carbon dioxide equivalent' refers to the carbon dioxide, plus the other greenhouse gases converted mathematically to a carbon dioxide standard. Professor Keith Shine, at Reading University, was reported to have calculated this figure at 425 ppm for early 2006 – already beyond the likely danger threshold.[8] In June 2013, the carbon dioxide equivalent was at 478 ppm, according to Massachusetts Institute of Technology's Professor Ron Prinn.[9] That's a rise of one-eighth since 2006.

"What's not appreciated is that there are a whole lot of other greenhouse gases (GHGs) that have fundamentally changed the composition of our atmosphere since pre-industrial time: methane, nitrous oxide, chlorofluorocarbons (CFCs) and hydrofluorocarbons. The screen of your laptop is probably manufactured in Taiwan, Japan, and Eastern China by a process that releases nitrogen trifluoride – release of 1 ton of nitrogen trifluoride is equivalent to 16,800 tons of CO_2."[10]

Methane concentrations in the atmosphere by 2013 were more than two and a half times greater than before 1750, at 1,824 parts per billion, while carbon dioxide alone at 396 parts per million was 142% greater and nitrous oxide, 325.9 parts per billion, was 121% higher.[11]

Emissions of greenhouse gases must be zero by 2200, warned the Tyndall Centre for Climate Change Research in its *Climate Change on the Millennial Timescale* [12] report for the UK's Environment Agency.[13] The report, predicting likely changes to the year 3000, drew attention to the risk of sudden, dramatic climatic shifts which could happen long after emissions have stopped:

"Abrupt changes may be triggered many decades before they actually occur. Even after emissions have completely ceased there is still a legacy from decades past – a 'sleeping giant' in the climate system."[14]

Politicians and corporations, with a few exceptions like former US presidential candidate Al Gore, take no notice. They may express intentions to force emissions cuts, but little happens.

Carbon trading is often regarded as a means to reduce emissions. Carbon trading allows organisations to sell unused portions of their 'allowances' of carbon dioxide to those whose emissions are greater than their allocation, and in the European Union a carbon trading scheme for heavy industries began at the start of 2005. The scheme had little impact because the allowances doled out by the EU, for free, were too large and thus many polluters had no need to buy in extra pollution permits. Greenhouse gas emissions continued to rise, and emissions trading became another arm of the unsustainably inflated financial derivatives market. An inter-agency report in the USA, published in January 2011, stated confidently that the US Commodity Futures Trading Commission (responsible for the emissions 'market') could rely on its enhanced authority in the Wall Street Reform and Consumer Protection Act to regulate the carbon derivatives market in an effective manner.[15] That fails to reassure me. As journalist Jeremy Warner put it,[16]

> "...the carbon market is based on lack of delivery, of an invisible substance, to no one. Since the market revolves around creating carbon credits, or finding carbon reduction projects whose benefits can then be sold to those with a surplus of emissions, it is entirely intangible".

This market in invisibles is, he said, "wide open to abuse and scams".

The carbon market failed to curb emissions. Countries like the UK reported nominal emissions cuts, achieved as a result of industrial relocations to economies with cheaper labour forces, notably China.

Banks have lost interest. At least ten banks in London had closed or shrunk their emissions trading operations by November 2013.[17] Between 2009 and 2013 there was a 70% fall in the number of London-based carbon traders, the Climate Markets & Investors Association reported.[18] Too many permits were issued, and the cost of buying them collapsed. Freedom to carry on polluting.

The Coalition government in the UK prioritised economic growth above emissions curbs. The European Union Commission expended effort in 2014 to try and force the UK government to stop compensating firms for the costs of emissions permits [19] Chancellor George Osborne introduced a scheme to reimburse some companies for up to 80% of the costs of the carbon price floor [20] and the emissions trading scheme. The EU Commission cited rules prohibiting state aid, except in sectors such as iron and steel, chemicals, plastics and paper, where an agreement covers the whole EU. Industry leaders in the high-energy sectors not covered by EU-wide agreement, such as cement, gypsum, ceramics and glass, made the usual complaints that taxing emissions damages their competitiveness and their future investment plans.

The logic of imposing emissions payments with one chancellory hand and trying to reimburse the bulk of those payments with the other hand reflects the triumph of style of over substance, of publicising financial penalties for emissions while aiming to subsidise heavily, with public money, those same payments, to promote business as usual.

Meanwhile, the Intergovernmental Panel on Climate Change continues to explain the risks of paradigm shifts in Earth's climates. *Climate Change 2014*, published by the IPCC's Working Group II on March 31st 2014, listed key risks as

- Storm surges, coastal flooding and sea level rise
- Inland flooding
- Breakdown of infrastructure networks and critical services such as electricity, water supply, health and emergency services
- Extreme heat
- Food insecurity and breakdown of food systems linked to warming, drought, flooding, precipitation variability and extremes
- Loss of rural livelihoods due to insufficient drinking and irrigation water, reduced agricultural productivity (especially by producers with little capital in semi-arid regions)
- Loss of marine and coastal ecosystems and biodiversity, affecting fishing communities notably in the tropics and the Arctic
- Loss of terrestrial and inland water ecosystems and biodiversity

Even the super-rich will be affected by changes such as these, because their favoured haunts will not escape. Rising seas will swamp low-lying tropical islands. Melting snows in the mountains will launch avalanches. Gated communities are as vulnerable as slums to severe climate events.

Climate change cannot be reduced to a simple action-reaction equation:

> "Understanding future vulnerability, exposure, and response capacity of interlinked human and natural systems is challenging due to the number of interacting social, economic, and cultural factors, which have been incompletely considered to date. These factors include wealth and its distribution across society, demographics, migration, access to technology and information, employment patterns, the quality of adaptive responses, societal values, governance structures, and institutions to resolve conflicts."
> -- IPCC Working Group II, *Climate Change 2014*, p.11

We are stumbling, blinkered, into the unknown. Will governments take note of Working Group II's opinion that "many estimates [of the economic costs of climate change] do not account for catastrophic changes, tipping points, and many other factors"? Will governments also heed the advice that "Indigenous, local and traditional knowledge systems and practices, including indigenous peoples' holistic view of community and environment, are a major resource for adapting to climate change"?

HURRICANES AND MELTING ICE

Surface seawater at 27 degrees C (80 degrees F) puts enough heat energy in the atmosphere to trigger a hurricane.[21] The hotter the water is, the greater the potential energy. Hurricanes start in tropical latitudes, where the ocean water is warm. The top 300 metres of the world's oceans warmed about 0.5 degree C between

1965 and 2005, during which time the destructive power of North Atlantic hurricanes doubled. The Mexican tourist resort of Cancún suffered from this power in 2005 when hurricane Wilma blew its beach – its main attraction for tourists – completely away. Wind and water both erode topsoil, which is being destroyed at least ten times faster than the natural replacement rate.[22]

The top 300 metres of so of the oceans are only a small part of the story, though. Scientists have discovered that, since the millennium, deep ocean water is heating much faster than near the surface. That heat can escape only in a few instances where deep water mixes with surface water, and so everywhere else the heat builds up and up.

Methane leaking from melting permafrost is another powerful greenhouse gas, over a 20-year time span some 86 times more potent than carbon dioxide.[23] Quite apart from the effects on global climates, methane is a light gas which can cause ships to sink and aircraft to crash. Ship disappearances in the 'Bermuda Triangle' have been blamed on the anti-buoyancy effect of methane.[24]

Arctic sea ice melting has multiple impacts, according to Dr Jeff Masters, meteorological director of the Weather Underground blog www.wunderground.com. He put it this way:[25]

"The dramatic loss of Arctic sea ice in recent years has created a fundamental new change in the atmospheric circulation in the Northern Hemisphere that has sped up sea ice loss and is affecting fall and winter weather across most of the Northern Hemisphere, according to several recent studies. Arctic sea ice loss peaks in September and October, exposing a large area of open water that heats the air above it. This extra heat has helped drive September-November air temperatures in the Arctic to 1 degree C or more above average over about half of the depth of the lower atmosphere. This deep layer of warm air has grown less dense and expanded, pushing the top of the troposphere (the lower atmosphere) higher. The result has been a decrease in the pressure gradient (the difference in pressure) between the North Pole and mid latitudes. With not as much difference in pressure to try and equalize, the jet stream has slowed down in the

Arctic, creating a major change in the atmospheric circulation for the Northern Hemisphere."

The previous atmospheric pattern, the North Atlantic Oscillation, was present at times but shared the Arctic region with a new pattern, the Arctic Dipole. The Dipole has high pressure over the North American Arctic and low pressure over the Eurasian Arctic, resulting in winds blowing from south to north, bringing more heat into the Arctic, a positive feedback further speeding the disappearance of ice.

The pallor of ice reflects solar radiation back out of the atmosphere, in so far as the rapidly thickening blanket of carbon dioxide and other greenhouse gases permits. Dark ocean, in contrast, absorbs radiation, thus quickening the warming process, and accelerating the rise in sea level. During the 20th century, sea levels rose between 4.4 and 8.8 inches,[26] and the rise was concentrated in the latter years of the century. Paradoxically, warmer oceans might make the British Isles colder. The rush of cold fresh water from melting glaciers leads to changes in the pattern of ocean currents. In the North Atlantic, that means a dilution of the Gulf Stream that warms the UK and Ireland.

The strength of North Atlantic currents decreased by around 30% between 1992 and 2004, according to research published in the journal *Nature*[27] in 2005. Measuring Atlantic water flows at 25 degrees North had been done for only 50 years, and so there was not a longer-term historical context in which to assess the findings, but they did appear to herald a certain chill. Perhaps the British climate would become more like that of Newfoundland and Labrador in Canada, at roughly the same latitudes, between 50 and 60 degrees North. January in Labrador has day temperatures around −10 to −15 degrees C (14 to 5 degrees F). The summer is short, and in July the temperature at the coast may reach 10 degrees C (50 degrees F), up to 15 degrees (59 degrees F) inland. Over most of Labrador, half of the 800 millimetres (31 to 32 inches) of precipitation falls as snow. The whole province of Newfoundland

and Labrador covers 156,483 square miles but only 513,000 people live there, just nine per square mile. The harsh climate deters settlement.

Reporting in 2013, the Intergovernmental Panel on Climate Change indicated that the Atlantic Meridional Overturning Circulation, of which the Gulf Stream is part, is likely to weaken by 20% to 44% by 2100, disrupting the weather patterns we have come to accept as 'normal' and cooling British temperatures by about 1 degree C (1.8 degrees F).

We do not know the extent to which a cooling Gulf Stream would be offset by higher air temperatures resulting from greenhouse gases, or exactly how these changes would affect our environments and activities, but the prospects of sudden shifts mean that we must be prepared to make rapid and drastic adjustments in our economies and lifestyles.

DESERTS AND WATER SHORTAGES

Since the end of the last Ice Age some 10,000 to 12,000 years ago, goats and other domesticated livestock have destroyed vegetation, leading to erosion, soil infertility, and the expansion of deserts. Earth may be the blue planet, but supplies of fresh water are under threat, and modern agriculture is more than a little to blame. Worldwide, agriculture consumes about 70% of all the water that is extracted from rivers or siphoned from aquifers.

After agriculture, power generation is the next biggest user of water: each kilowatt hour (kWh) needs 25 gallons of water, mainly for cooling. Future demand for water is set to rise in line with population growth, but current extraction rates are already far too high, raising the spectre of diminishing supplies. A third of the land on Earth is desert, and the amount expands every year. The reasons are many and complex but include both human-induced climate change and excessive water abstraction. Settlements in arid areas require water to be pumped up from aquifers, depleting them and hastening water shortages.

Australia's Murray-Darling river system, draining 400,000 square miles of Queensland, New South Wales, Victoria and South Australia, ran low in 2005, 60% lower than in the recent past. Decades of irrigation followed by drought had made soils saline, less fertile year on year. The Murray-Darling region suffered different problems in 2010, torrential rains that damaged crops and washed away soil. Perplexed farmers became angry when the government issued plans to cut by 30% the amount of water that may be drawn from the rivers for crops and livestock. There are farmers who regard global warming as a myth, on the grounds that if weather forecasters cannot predict one or two days ahead accurately, how can they possibly know what the climate will be like in 10, 20 or 30 years? Yet the farmers of the Murray-Darling region already experience water shortages separated by occasional and catastrophic water gluts, and soils that are becoming exhausted. Professor Barry Brook, an environmental scientist at the University of Adelaide, commented on the BraveNewClimate website, [28] "...concern over global warming has cooled precisely as its impacts in the Murray Darling Basin conspire with greed and stupidity to cause a problem that will be evident in foreclosures, suicide and despair in coming years".

The Australian government responded to the environmental damage in the river plains by creating, in 2008, the Murray-Darling Basin Authority (MDBA). The plan formulated by the authority, published in 2011 and signed into law in November 2012, is to cut water extractions by 2,750 gigalitres[29] a year over a seven-year period. This appears a compromise deal which is unlikely to satisfy the public, farmers reliant on irrigation, or environmentalists. The MDBA itself says that the long-term health of the whole system is at risk:

"Enormous strain is now being placed on the Basin's communities, industries and natural environments by a combination of drought and

flood, emerging changes in climate, population growth and the impact of past water allocation decisions. Many of the Basin's rivers and groundwater systems are stressed and over allocated."
-- Murray-Darling Basin Authority[30]

THE AMU DARYA IN CENTRAL ASIA

In Central Asia the Amu Darya river flows north into the Aral Sea no longer, but peters out in the Kyzyl Kum desert of Uzbekistan. This desert merges with Turkmenistan's Kara Kum desert to the west, creating a harsh environment. The Aral Sea, deprived of the water of the Amu Darya, is disappearing. This former inland sea, about as big as Ireland in an atlas published in 1962, shrank to half that size by 1992. "Freshwater flow into the Aral Sea is about 25 percent that of the 1960s," said the National Geographic Association's *Orbit*, a book of photographs of the Earth taken from space. "The area of the Aral Sea has shrunk by nearly 50 per cent, and its salinity has increased four times," continued the report.[31] Loose salts left as the water receded, mixed with pesticides and fertilisers from formerly irrigated farmland growing cotton, form a "toxic dust" that makes people ill with lung cancer, intestinal illnesses and respiratory problems. The dust deposits are visible from space.

By 2013, the Aral Sea had reduced to three lakes, covering less than a quarter of its size in the 1960s. Images on Google Earth, taken in April 2013, show a wasteland where hardly anything grows. Winds deposit salts and sands, from the dried sea bed, far over the land for hundreds of kilometres, killing vegetation including crops and pasture. This loss of fresh water is a disaster for humans, agriculture and ecosystems. Photos show desolate salt flats, where once there was a fishing industry. No water, no fish. Clean drinking water is now scarce.

The Interstate Commission for Water Co-ordination, representing Kazakhstan, Tajikistan, Turkmenistan, Uzbekistan and the Kyrgyz Republic, the five former Soviet republics in the Amu Darya drainage basin, dates from the early 1990s but apart from in the now disconnected North Aral Sea has been unable to reverse the dramatic desertification resulting from the sea's shrinkage.

The North Aral, into which the Syr Darya flows, has benefited from restoration work initiated by the government of Kazakhstan. More water from the Syr Darya reaches the sea, following works to cut losses from irrigation channels. A dam, the Dike Kokaral, has been constructed in Kazakhstan to stop water from the North Aral Sea from flowing into the formerly much larger South Aral Sea, unless deliberately released. Since the dam was completed in 2005, the sea area has expanded from 2,550 square kilometres to 3,300 square kilometres, and its depth has increased from 30 metres to 42 metres. Fish are surviving in the waters, and fishing as an industry has been able to restart.

Plans for a second dam, to bring the waters back to the former port of Aralsk, are gathering dust waiting for money to finance it, though. Down to the south, there is no comparable scheme to save the disappearing South Aral Sea, which lies half in Kazakhstan and half in Uzbekistan. For the government of Uzbekistan, water extraction from the Amu Darya to irrigate crops, notably cotton, continues to take precedence over environmental protection. The dry sea bed has another economic use for Uzbekistan – as an oil and gas field.

CNPC (China National Petroleum Corporation) and Uzbekistan's state oil and gas company, Uzbekneftegaz, made a deal in 2004, and two years later Lukoil, Petronas and Korea National Oil Corporation joined them to sign a production sharing agreement with the Uzbek government. In 2008 construction began on the Uzbek section of the Central Asia-China Gas Pipeline, which was completed in December 2009.[32] The following year Uzbekistan agreed to send 10 billion cubic metres of natural gas to China every year.

Water had no chance in an economic competition with oil and gas.

CHINA'S BILLION TONNE WATER DIVERSION PROJECT

In China, desperate scrabbling for more water includes desalination, collecting and melting snow, and myriad water engineering projects – reservoirs, canals, aqueducts – which are expensive to construct and maintain.

Falling water tables hasten the conversion of farmland into desert. Around Beijing the water table is reported to have been falling about five feet every year.[33] Since the millennium, more governments and local authorities have been considering desalination as an answer to shortages of fresh water. China's largest desalination plant, near Tianjin in northern China, supplies about 200,000 cubic metres of water daily, but it is expensive to produce in terms of both fuel (coal) and emissions. Cost depends on numerous factors, but in 2013 was typically around 30p to 60p a cubic metre, before transportation. The coal-fired combined power and desalination plant worsens the notorious Beijing smogs, and the desalinated water tends to come out of taps brown with the rust it has scrubbed from pipes.

The Tianjin plant cost over £1.1 billion, generates 4,000MW, and uses Israeli desalination equipment.[34] The cost of production is already twice the market price of drinking water, but the deteriorating supply is pushing up market prices to levels impossible for the poor to afford, if they are also to eat.

Beijing's population long ago outran the water supply. By 2013 the 20.7 million people of the city, its factories and businesses, were using 3.6 billion cubic metres, but only 2.1 billion cubic metres could be extracted from local surface and groundwater supplies. Almost 40% of Beijing's water had to be found elsewhere. The city's population is growing by about half a million a year, while the water supply is shrinking.

The national government looked to giant engineering projects to solve the problem, under the name of the South-North Water Diversion Project, on which construction began in 2002. The aim is to transfer one billion tonnes of water annually from southern China to the dusty northern plains where Beijing has mushroomed. The first phase, carrying water from the Yangtze in Jiangsu province to the eastern central coastal province of Shandong, opened on December 10th 2013.[35]

The initial cost estimates were about US$62 billion, 40% of which has been raised from banks. This is not a project with a final cost, however, because each stretch of canal or pipe creates new problems of pollution and insufficient supply in the water donor regions, so new dams, new treatment works, have to be built – and it will all have to be maintained, indefinitely. The diverted water is expected to cost about 10 yuan, $1.6 or £1 a cubic metre (1,000 litres). If it were to be much cheaper than that, it would not be possible to maintain the mammoth engineering works.

The city of Xiangyang, on the Han river, benefits from a fairly clean water supply. The water diversion project will change that: about 30% of water in the Danjiangkou reservoir, which flows into the Han river, will be diverted away to the north. Xiangyang will suffer a drastic water loss.

Climate change did not enter the flow calculations for the diversion project, which were based on average flows between the 1950s and the early 1990s. Since then droughts and floods have become more frequent, and during droughts Xiangyang can ill afford to lose water to other parts of China. The Han river, which supplies some 11 million people, flows into the Yangtze, the main water artery for 400 millions.

China's rivers are disappearing so fast that diversion schemes risk becoming ineffective money pits. China's first national water census has found 22,909 rivers, when before 1990 maps showed some 50,000.[36] The dried-up Wanquan in Beijing is one of the dying rivers, and the saddest aspect is that if industrial growth and city expansion had been controlled, and if water conservation had been paramount, China's water shortages would be less frightening.

China is relying largely on the Yangtze and its tributaries, like the Han, to rescue it from severe water scarcity. The Three Gorges Dam in Hubei province is on the Yangtze – the Europeanised name for the Changjiang -- down-river from the industrial city of Chongqing. The dam, site of the world's largest hydro-electric power scheme with 22,500 MW capacity, is 181 metres – 588 feet – high. Yet the prize of electricity comes at an unknown, possibly catastrophic cost. The weight of the deep water behind the dam, in the reservoir stretching for 370 miles, could increase seismic shudders, even major earthquakes. Sediment is accumulating, blocking sluice gates, and without constant dredging this could lead eventually to dam failure. Sedimentation could also increase the risk of flooding upstream from the dam. The man-made sea covers heavily polluted industrial sites (as well as beautiful landscapes) and pollutants and rubbish entering from upstream accumulate in the waters, to form what the International Rivers Organisation calls "a festering bog of effluent, silt, industrial pollutants and rubbish".[37] Downstream, river flow is reduced, damaging fisheries.

The lake behind the dam covers 365 towns and fertile farmland. About 1.2 million people were relocated, often to strange and uncongenial surroundings.

The dams are not enough to relieve China's water deficit. Ground water pumps are not enough. China's decision to turn to desalination shows that it has run out of simpler options, because desalination is an expensive, energy-inefficient way to make 'fresh' water.

For China, home to one person in every five on the planet, the depletion of water resources means food security declines year on year. In 2013 China imported 22.8 million tons of grain, nearly double the amount in 2012,[38] and self-sufficiency in grains is below 90%. One hectare in every five of China's 130 million hectares of arable land is contaminated, particularly by cadmium, nickel and arsenic. The pollution is severe in the rice growing areas of the south, and in the deltas of the Yangtze and Pearl rivers.

So China looked for farmland in countries elsewhere, in South America, Africa, Central Asia – and in the Ukraine.

Ukraine has great agricultural potential. In 2013 a company operating in the Ukraine, KSG Agro, signed a huge deal worth $2.6 billion [39] with China's Xinjiang Production and Construction Corporation to rent up to 3 million hectares for 50 years, although KSG itself does not control anything like that amount of land, only 94,000 hectares in March 2015.

The China-Ukraine deal raises so many questions about the control of land and thus of food. KSG Agro SA is a Luxembourg-registered company controlled by Ukrainian businessman Sergiy Kasianov, who as at September 17th 2014 owned 65.65% of the shares through his Swiss-based company ICD Investments SA. Generali OFE, a Polish subsidiary of the Italian insurance group Generali, owned 10.001% and other investors the remaining 24.35%. As both Luxembourg and Switzerland are well-known as tax havens, the people of Ukraine would be unlikely to see, as of right, profits from the deal.

Ukraine itself is far from a stable entity. More than a fifth of KSG Agro's land, 22,400 hectares, is in Crimea, which Russia annexed in March 2014. Most of the rest is in eastern Ukraine, where there is vocal popular support for joining Russia, or at least co-operating closely with Russia.

Ukraine also supplies arms to China, the latest at the time of writing being advanced landing craft air cushions purchased from Ukroboronprom, according to defence analysts Janes.

The ousting of president Viktor Yanukovich, a strong ally of Russia, in February 2014 and the installation of a more pro-European government suggests that Western interests want to interrupt the eastwards flows of food and arms to China, and probably to Russia too. The government change, and the fomented unrest, has a lot more to do with global resource competition than with peace and prosperity for the Ukrainians.

The crisis in Ukraine is a precursor of future conflicts over food, paralleling conflicts over oil and gas.

China will be ever more desperate for food, because lack of water and land loss resulting from urbanisation could cause crop yields to fall by 14% to 23% between 2010 and 2050, predicted Lin Erda [40] of the Chinese Academy of Agricultural Sciences. The population is growing by some 6 to 7 million a year, creating a double squeeze. Environmental degradation in China prompted American geography professor Joshua Muldavin, of Sarah Lawrence College, to say:

> "China's fabulous growth since the 1980s was achieved through environmental destruction and social and economic polarisation which now threaten its continuation." [41]

He added that emerging rural unrest, a consequence of the rush to industrial expansion and the low priority given to rural communities, is a challenge to the legitimacy of China's rapid economic growth. [42]

CLIMATE CHANGE DENIAL

Climate deniers have not given up their campaigns, which are often generously funded by industrialists and the neo-conservative tendency. One man, Lord Lawson of Blaby, is probably the best known climate change sceptic in the UK, often included in discussions to give 'balance' to a debate that would otherwise be dominated by scientists who accept that climate change is happening. Lord Lawson is not a scientist but the former Conservative Chancellor of the Exchequer Nigel Lawson, who held the influential position between 1983 and 1989, when the late Margaret Thatcher was Prime Minister.

Lord Lawson is an evangelist for fracking. His many contributions in the House of Lords include promotion of shale gas extraction in the UK, which on May 8th 2014 he called a "massive opportunity":

> "Does the Minister agree with the committee that unless the government streamline the regulatory system and unless they get their act together, this massive opportunity will not be realised?" [43]

47

In 2009 Lord Lawson founded the Global Warming Policy Foundation as a charity to disseminate data and opinions which the foundation's supporters felt should be aired. Foundation director Dr Benny Peiser is a social anthropologist with a PhD in cultural studies, who until 2010 lectured in the School of Sport and Exercise Sciences at Liverpool John Moores University. He left to become a visiting fellow at the University of Buckingham, which he combines with directing the foundation. (The University of Buckingham, which is privately funded, set up a new Centre for Extractive Energy Studies in October 2013.)

There is another link between the University of Buckingham and the Global Warming Policy Foundation in the person of foundation trustee Sir Martin Jacomb, who was the Chancellor of the university between 1998 and 2010. Sir Martin was a director of the Bank of England, 1986-95 and deputy chair of Barclays Bank, 1985-93.

The eight trustees of the foundation comprise four lords including Lord Lawson, a bishop, a baroness and two knights. The list is very top drawer and links government and industry. Lord Turnbull, a non-executive director of Prudential, British Land Co and Frontier Economics Ltd,[44] is a prime example. As Andrew Turnbull he was Principal Private Secretary to the Prime Minister, 1988-92; then Permanent Secretary to HM Treasury, 1998-2002; and Secretary of the Cabinet and Head of the Home Civil Service, 2002-05.

Further adding to the respectability, there is an academic advisory council of 26, all male. In fact at the time of writing, the sole woman among the trustees or academics was a trustee, the Conservative-turned-LibDem peer Baroness Nicholson, who is better known as a politician than as either a climate change sceptic or activist.[45]

The academic advisers in spring 2014 included only two meteorologists or climate scientists, Professors Lennart Bengtsson and Richard Lindzen. Lennart Bengtsson was listed as a research fellow at the University of Reading, where his research project was 'global energy studies (production and use of renewable, fossil and nuclear energy)'. His research interests include 'energy balance in present and future climates' and 'natural climate variability and climate predictability'. Professor Bengtsson resigned from the advisory board in May 2014, citing pressure from other meteorologists.

Richard Lindzen used to be Alfred P Sloan Professor of Meteorology at the Massachusetts Institute of Technology, but left in May 2013 to join the Cato Institute, which is 'dedicated to the principles of individual liberty, limited government, free markets and peace'. He remained on the advisory board at the time of writing.

The economist Professor David Henderson, chair of the editorial advisory council, is also on the advisory council of the Institute of Economic Affairs, which works to promote markets as the best medium of solving economic and social problems, a similar aim to the Cato Institute in the USA.

So the Global Warming Policy Foundation is overwhelmingly male, non-meteorological, and free market. The academic specialisms of other advisers hint at the policy emphasis, subjects such as biochemistry, economics, electrical engineering, geology, geophysics, medical entomology, metallurgy, mining geology, and transport. The mix spells industrial growth, not carbon reduction.

As an education charity, the foundation is restricted by the regulations of the Charity Commission, i.e. it cannot get involved in political campaigns. Thus in May 2014 the foundation announced it was to create a non-charitable campaigning offshoot, the Global Warming Policy Forum. Will it try to convince us that the free market will blow to the rescue and let us carry on drilling, mining, burning, with impunity?

FUNDAMENTALS

In the years around the millennium in the USA, an alliance of fundamental Christians and international energy corporations had the ear of Republican opinion formers including advisers to President George W Bush. A paper called 'Environmental effects of increased atmospheric carbon dioxide' by Arthur R Robinson, Sallie L Baliunas, Willie Soon and Zachary W Robinson,[46] writing for the Oregon Institute of Science and Medicine, and the George C Marshall Institute, Washington, was published in January 1998.[47] The paper's premise was that increased concentrations of carbon dioxide are good because they promote abundant plant growth, thus increasing food supply:

> "Greenhouse gases cause plant life, and the animal life that depends on it, to thrive. What mankind is doing is liberating carbon from beneath the Earth's surface and putting it into the atmosphere, where it is available for conversion into living organisms."

The authors rejected a link between greenhouse gases and rising surface air temperatures, arguing that temperature changes are the result of fluctuations in solar activity. They said, reassuringly,

> "We… need not worry about environmental calamities, even if the current long-term natural warming trend continues. The Earth has been much warmer during the past 3000 years without catastrophic effects. Warmer weather extends growing seasons and generally improves the habitability of colder regions."

According to their vision,

> "As coal, oil and natural /gas are used to feed and lift from poverty vast numbers of people across the globe, more CO_2 will be released into the atmosphere. This will help to maintain and improve the health, longevity, prosperity and productivity of all people."

The simplicity of this vision, the absence of references to any other consequences of rising CO_2 concentrations – possibilities such as flooding of low-lying prime farmland as a result of thermal expansion of the oceans, and changes in oceans' thermohaline[48] circulation, for example in the Gulf Stream current that warms the sea, and thus the climate, of maritime north-west Europe – made me wonder about the Oregon Institute of Science and Medicine and the George C Marshall Institute.

General George C Marshall (1880 to 1959) was Chief of Staff of the US Military during World War 2, when he supported the development of nuclear weapons. From 1947 to 1949 he was Secretary of State, and he was the moving force behind the plan to reconstruct war-ravaged Europe, the programme known ever since as the Marshall Plan. The institute that bears his name was founded in Washington DC in 1984, and is reported by Source Watch (www.sourcewatch.org) to have received funds originating in huge industrial conglomerates like the USA's ExxonMobil, which vies with the Anglo-Dutch Royal Dutch Shell for top spot in world oil company rankings.

The institute's work centres on issues it sees as vital to national defence, such as the colonisation of space. Matthew Crawford, who was executive director of the institute for five months in 2001, said later[49] that the job felt illiberal, as he had to come up with "the best arguments money could buy", which meant that the tie he wore "started to feel like the mark of a slave". The chief executive officer at the time of writing is William O'Keefe, a former executive vice-president of the American Petroleum Institute.

The Oregon Institute of Science and Medicine, from which the paper called 'Environmental effects of increased atmospheric carbon dioxide' emanated, is an independent centre supported by donations and commercial earnings. Dr Arthur Robinson founded the Oregon Institute of Science and Medicine after moving to the state in 1980. Until 1978 he was scientific director of the Linus Pauling Institute, but disagreed with Pauling's certainty that vitamin C is an important anti-cancer agent. The disagreement became acrimonious and led to litigation, which secured Robinson a settlement that enabled him to start an independent life.

Independent scientists are indispensable. James Lovelock, who developed Gaia theory of Earth as a single self-regulating system with physical, chemical, biological and human components, is an independent scientist. Albert Einstein was a patent clerk when he wrote papers that revolutionised physics. Gregor Mendel, so important to the science of genetics, was a monk. Even Isaac Newton was at home, not at Cambridge University, when he worked out the principles of differential calculus. The problem now is not independence but quasi-independence, supported financially by rich industrial and commercial funders intent upon their own perceived self-interest.

'Evidence-based policy' is one of the smokescreens drifting in front of our eyes. Politicians, like people in general, are inclined to select only the evidence which supports their pre-existing beliefs. Early in the 21st century, policymakers in the USA paid little attention to research coming out of the government's own laboratories. The Geophysical Fluid Dynamics Laboratory (GFDL), based at Princeton University in New Jersey, is part of the National Oceanic and Atmospheric Administration within the US Department of Commerce. Yet the results of its climate change modelling were startlingly different from the Bush administration's assumptions. A paper in 2004 titled 'Climate impact of quadrupling CO_2: an overview of GFDL climate model results'[50] suggested that doubling CO_2 levels in the atmosphere would result in a major disappearance of sea ice. Thermally driven rise in sea levels would probably continue for centuries after the atmospheric CO_2 stopped rising. If current CO_2 concentrations quadrupled, sea levels around the world would rise by a foot after 100 years, nearly six feet after 500 years, due to thermal expansion alone. Melting of continental ice sheets would multiply this many times. Disappearance of the Greenland ice sheet could cause a 23 feet rise in sea level, and disappearance of Antarctica's ice sheet, over 235 feet. The USA would suffer. More than half of Florida would sink below the waters if sea levels rose 26 feet, so would the whole Mississippi delta, and the eastern seaboard.

The GFDL research also drew attention to the decline of thermohaline circulations such as the Gulf Stream. At a quadrupling of CO_2 the Gulf Stream would disappear. At a doubling of CO_2 the current would probably weaken to less than half its present strength, and then recover, but only after several centuries. Summer drying in mid latitudes would be another probable catastrophe. With a doubling of CO_2 most of the central states in the USA could experience a 30% to 40% drop in soil moisture between June and August. At quadruple concentrations, the decline in soil moisture could exceed 50% over huge swathes of the USA. Greater incidence of high humidity would increase the discomfort of higher temperatures for people and animals.

The GFDL's forecasting work indicates that there would be less land on which to live and to produce food, and much of it would be very dry in summer. People would be uncomfortable in the heat, and would often feel that they were living in a greenhouse. The laboratory's work has been carried out on behalf of the US government, but the findings were not accepted by the George W Bush administration. Of course it is naïve to expect political administrations to act contrary to the self-believed interests of their funders, and that is where the so-called democratic process hits a massive stone wall, a wall which expands as income and economic inequalities gape wider. The inequalities mean that the financial clout to influence policymaking is concentrated in fewer and fewer hands.

In California, the weapons-oriented Lawrence Livermore National Laboratory, part of the Department of Energy's National Nuclear Security Administration, predicted in 2005 that Earth would warm by 8 degrees C, 14.5 degrees F, by 2300 unless carbon dioxide emissions were slashed immediately.[51] Atmospheric carbon dioxide would nearly quadruple from 380 parts per million to over 1,420 parts per million. The Arctic could suffer temperature rises of over 20 degrees C, and the sea ice would disappear. Eventually, around 80% of the carbon dioxide would be taken up by sea water, making it much more acidic and harmful to marine life. The oceans, which would cover more of the Earth than they do now, because of the melting ice pouring in to them, could become hostile to aquatic life.

This Lawrence Livermore research used a coupled climate cycle and carbon cycle model. Models are simpler than the realities they try to represent, so the future they indicate is very unlikely to be closely accurate, but they are the best tools we have for forward planning.

The US aircraft carrier of state is not yet for turning away from a nexus of economic growth and weapons supremacy. Nuclear weapons are the Livermore speciality, including research into nuclear fusion, but other work includes underground coal gasification and carbon capture and storage, an acknowledgement that fossil fuels remain at the heart of US policy, and that little will be done to limit emissions – because even if technologies trim emission percentages, expansion of economic activity counteracts the reductions.

This way we reach the cliff edge sooner.

---

[1] See www.arch.ox.ac.uk/TOBA.html, the Oxford University School of Archaeology, accessed November 18th 2010, and 'Toba supervolcano and climate change' by Jim Andrews, www.accuweather.com/en/weather-blogs/andrews/toba-supervolcano-and-climate-change/37113, September 13th 2010.

[2] Independent Evaluation Group of the World Bank, *Hazards of Nature, Risks to Development: an IEG Evaluation of World Bank Assistance for Natural Disasters*, April 21st 2006. Extract is from the Executive Summary.

[3] Discussion paper published January 31st 2006.

[4] Brian Goodwin, 'From control to participation' in *Resurgence* No.201, July/August 2000.

[5] www.hm-treasury.gov.uk/media/F7A/5F/climatechange_sin.pdf

[6] Parts per million.

[7] Dr Meinshausen moved to the Potsdam Institute for Climate Impact Research in 2006 and was researching there, as well as at the University of Melbourne, Australia, at the time of writing in 2014. 'Meeting the EU 2degC climate target: global and regional emission implications' by M G J den Elzen and M Meinshausen, *Climate Policy* 6, 2006, pps. 545-564.

[8] Professor Shine's calculation is reported in 'Greenhouse gases are already past threshold that spells disaster' by Michael McCarthy, *The Independent*, February 11th 2006.

[9] '400 ppm CO_2? Add other GHGs and it's equivalent to 478 ppm', by Professor Ron Prinn, oceans.mit.edu/featured-stories/5-questions-mits-ron-prinn-400-ppm-threshold, June 6th 2013, accessed April 21st 2014.

[10] Prinn, op.cit. p.1

[11] World Meteorological Association, *Greenhouse Gas Bulletin* no.10, September 9th 2014, www.wmo.int/pages/mediacentre/press_releases/documents/1002_GHG_Bulletin.pdf

[12] *Climate Change on the Millennial Timescale*, report to the Environment Agency of Tyndall Centre Research Project T3.18, by Rachel Warren, Timothy Lenton, Marie-France Loutre, Mark S Williamson, Clare M Goodess, Matthew Swann, David R Cameron, Robert Hankin, Robert Marsh and John Shepherd, 2006.

[13] 'New science shows urgent action needed today on climate change', release from the Environment Agency and the Tyndall Centre, February 16th 2006.

[14] Ref. Warren *et. al.* as above.

[15] 'Oversight sufficient for US carbon derivatives market: report', www.platts.com/latest-news/coal/washington/oversight-sufficient-for-us-carbon-derivatives-8429015, January 19th 2011.

[16] 'Here comes the next bubble – carbon trading' by Jeremy Warner, http://blogs.telegraph.co.uk/finance/jeremywarner/100003851/here-comes-the-next-bubble-carbon-trading/, February 19th 2010.

[17] 'London banks quit carbon trading' by Jim Pickard and Ajay Makan, www.ft.com/cms/s/0/cbb749ba-506b-11e3-9f0d-00144feabdc0.html#axzz3EvA8X1fD, November 18th 2013.

[18] 'London banks quit carbon trading', op.cit.

[19] 'EU blow to UK energy-intensive companies' by Brian Groom, Andy Sharman and Alex Barker, www.ft.com/cms/s/0/2f9d78e6-c894-11e3-8976-00144feabdc0.html#axzz3EvA8X1fD, April 21st 2014.

[20] The carbon price floor (CPF) was a Coalition government policy for an additional tax on greenhouse gas emissions. It was supposed to be £15.70 per tonne of CO_2 equivalent in 2013-14, rising in steps to £30 in 2020-21 and £70 in 2030-31. The Chancellor backtracked in the March 2014 Budget, setting the level at £9.55 a tonne for 2014-15 and £18.08 until at least 2020.

[21] A hurricane is called a typhoon in the western Pacific north of the equator and a cyclone in the Indian Ocean.

[22] The USA National Academy of Sciences, in 'The lowdown on topsoil: it's disappearing' by Tom Paulson, Seattle Post-Intelligencer, www.seattlepi.com/national/article/The-lowdown-on-topsoil-It-s-disappearing-1262214.php, January 21st 2008.

[23] 'The tipping point in action: twice as much methane released due to seabed permafrost melting' by Christine Lepisto, November 26th 2013, www.treehugger.com/climate-change/tipping-point-action-twice-much-methane-released-due-seabed-permafrost-melting.html

[24] 'Methane gas in Bermuda Triangle', www.bermuda-attractions.com, introduces arguments for and against theories of methane causing boat and plane disappearances.

[25] Weather Underground, www.wunderground.com, December 11th2009.

[26] US Environmental Protection Agency, data updated August 19th2010.

[27] 'Slowing of the Atlantic Meridional Overturning Circulation at 25degN' by H Bryden, H Longworth and S Cunningham, *Nature* 2005 Vol.438 pps.655-657.

[28] 'Who crippled the Murray Darling Basin?' by Barry Brook, http://bravenewclimate.com/2010/10/18/who-crippled-the-murray-darling-basin, October 18th 2010.

[29] A gigalitre is one billion litres.

[30] mdba.gov.au, accessed April 23rd 2014.

[31] *Orbit: NASA Astronauts Photograph the Earth*, by Jay Apt, Michael Helfert and Justin Wilkinson, p.87, published by the National Geographic Society, 1996.

[32] 'CNPC in Uzbekistan', information from CNPC, http://classic.cnpc.com.cn/en/cnpcworldwide/uzbekistan/, accessed April 24th 2014.

[33] 'China's water crisis is an investment opportunity', www.seekingalpha.com/article/146151-china-s-water-crisis-is-an-investment-opportunity, June 30th 2009.

[34] 'Tianjin to have desalinated seawater as domestic water', June 4th 2010, formerly on www.china.org.cn/environment.

[35] 'China is so bad at conservation that it had to launch the most impressive water-pipeline ever' by Lily Kuo, http://journal.probeinternational.org/2014/03/17/china-is-so-bad-at-conservation-that-it-had-to-launch-the-most-impressive-water-pipeline-project-ever/, March 17th 2014.

[36] '28,000 rivers disappeared in China: what happened?' by Angel Hsu and William Miao, www.theatlantic.com/china/archive/2013/04/28-000-rivers-disappeared-in-china-what-happened/275365, April 29th 2013.

[37] 'Three Gorges Dam', undated, www.internationalrivers.org/campaigns/three-gorges-dam, accessed April 27th 2014.

[38] 'China imports 4% of the world's grain and that's still not enough' by Lily Kuo, http://qz.com/140994/china-imports-4-of-the-worlds-grain-and-thats-still-not-enough/, October 29th 2013.

[39] 'Ukraine to be China's largest overseas farmer', by Mandy Zuo, South China Morning Post, www.scmp.com/news/china/article/1314902/ukraine-become-chinas-largest-overseas-farmer-3m-hectare-deal, September 22nd 2013.

[40] 'China to plough extra 20% into agricultural production amid fears that climate change will spark food crisis', by Jonathan Watts, www.theguardian.com/environment/2009/mar/05/china-food-farming, March 5th2009.

[41] In 'The polluter pays: how environmental disaster is straining China's social fabric', www.ft.com/cms/s/0/e2e778ce-8ed8-11da-b752-0000779e2340.html#axzz3EvA8X1fD, January 27th 2006.

[42] 'China pours £70bn into rescuing its water supply', http://journal.probeinternational.org/2006/08/22/china-pours-a70bn-rescuing-its-water-supply-1/, August 22nd 2006.

[43] Hansard, May 8th 2014, col. 1578.

[44] The Parliamentary website www.parliament.uk/ has biographies of MPs and peers, including Lord Turnbull.

[45] Lists of trustees and members of the Editorial Advisory Council of the Global Warming Policy Foundation are on www.thegwpf.org/who-we-are/

[46] One of Arthur's sons.

[47] See 'Environmental effects of increased atmospheric carbon dioxide' by Arthur B Robinson, Noah E Robinson and Willie Soon, 1998, www.oism.org/pproject/s33p36.htm

[48] Ice sheet melt reduces salinity in the oceans.

[49] 'White-collar work is doomed: get your hands dirty' interview with Matthew Crawford by John-Paul Flintoff, *The Sunday Times*, January 2nd 2011. Mr Crawford's book *The Case for Working with your Hands* (Penguin 2011) argues that too many people go to university and that skilled craft work is the way ahead.

[50] www.gfdl.noaa.gov/~tk/climate_dynamics/climate_impact_webpage.html, dated May 7th 2004.

[51] 'Modeling of long-term fossil fuel consumption shows 15.5-degree hike in Earth's temperature', Lawrence Livermore National Laboratory, November 1st 2005. www.llnl.gov/PAO/news/news_releases/2005/NR-05-11-01p.html

CHAPTER 4
LAND AND FOOD AS WEAPONS

RESTRICTED ACCESS TO LAND

La Via Campesina is an international movement of small-scale family farmers, active in 73 countries and campaigning for a fair deal for subsistence and small-scale commercial farmers. Land reform is high on their agenda, because all over what we often used to call the 'third world' industrial agriculture has acquired, often in dubious ways, the best land on which to grow crops and raise livestock for export markets.

In the battle between small-scale producers and corporations' 'Big Agriculture', the corporations have the advantage of access to capital, but over most of the world public opinion is sceptical about the claimed benefits of industrial-scale farming. The business of tying farmers in to tight contracts leaves little scope for individual flexibility, or for communities to prioritise their own food security.

Early in 2014, some 16,000 landless rural workers marched in Brazil's capital, Brazilia, to demand land reform. Brazil is supposed to have a land resettlement programme, but in 2013 only 7,000 Brazilian families received land, while over 150,000 were squatting in temporary camps, approaching two-thirds of them in camps run by the MST, Movimento dos Trabalhadores Rurais Sem Terra or Landless Workers Movement.

But resettling small-scale farmers on land is a waste of time, according to many international banks and corporations, for whom there is little profit in farmers who breed their own seeds and who practise techniques like companion planting. Often these are female farmers, whose skills are routinely undervalued and who rarely have strong title to the land they work.

Multinational businesses and national governments do not like parallel economies, especially if they empower poor people. The Cuban Revolution's expropriation of lands owned by absentee landlords, notably the United Fruit Company, is a major cause of over 50 years of blockade and harassment by the United States, 90 miles away across the Strait of Florida. For 30 years, Soviet money subsidised the Cuban state, but after the collapse of the Soviet Union the financial flows and the Russian markets for sugar and rum dried up, and many Cubans became very hungry indeed.

The action taken by individuals and the state was to grow food, on rooftops, in pots, on wasteland, on former pasture, anywhere. As a consequence, Cubans have become expert in urban and organic agriculture. While Cuba's expertise in community food production grew, at the same time tourism was also expanding – and with it voracious demands for more and more food. The explosion in tourism since the mid-1990s brought in foreign exchange, but also heightened many Cubans' sense of exploitation. How come these pale visitors from the North (Canada and Europe, mainly, as the US government[1] stopped its nationals from travel to the island nation) could afford foreign holidays when they were just doing ordinary jobs? How come they had so many gadgets, so much cash and how come they could consume so much of the best food?

Bemused Cubans took much of tourists' 'wealth' at face value. The Western reliance on debt to fund current spending was not properly explained to them, the unsustainable looting of Earth's resources to create the appearance of economic growth was too often left unsaid. Instead of deconstructing the story of Western 'prosperity', the Cuban government clamped down on communications, but people listened to foreign radio stations and foreign TV (a lot of Latin American soap operas about affluent people with smart cars and stylish homes, not to mention plastic surgery enhancements).

In fact Cubans were living in a far more sustainable way than the visiting tourists. This was a matter of pride for some, but not for the majority. The absence of building materials to repair tumbledown homes, of vehicles to replace the 1950s American Buicks and Cadillacs from the Mafia era, was an everyday reminder of material poverty.

Raul Castro's government knows there is pressing need to produce more food. The solutions being tried include giving more marketing freedom to private farmers – who have always been part of the Cuban economy since the Revolution, each able to own up to 65 hectares, just over 160 acres – and to co-operatives. There are two types of farm co-op, either private farmers linking for services such as credit, access to machinery and training, or production co-ops where the land is held by the co-op and managed by an elected board of members. Most of the output of Cuban farming, except for the urban allotment-style gardens, *organoponicos*, used to be contracted to the state at fixed prices, but with a few state-retained exceptions such as tobacco and sugar, co-operatives are now taking over food wholesaling and retailing. Most prices are being liberated too, although not the dietary essentials of rice and beans.

And there is GM. GM (genetically modified) corn is grown in Cuba. This is a surprise, because it appears to conflict with the 'organic' policies in place since the financial pipelines from the Soviet Union were severed. The state arguments in favour are that the state itself has developed GM varieties, so no multinational corporations are involved; one corn variety is resistant to the palomilla moth, which is a serious pest; and Cuba is in urgent need of more food, because – tourism again – up to 70% is imported. The 2.7 million tourists arriving every year want to eat well, and although they bring vital foreign currency, they are competing for food with 11.3 million Cubans.

The Cuban state has land at its disposal to offer to new farmers, but is very short of investment funds. Even so, opportunities for new entrants to farming do exist. In the UK, farmland is a desirable asset class, priced far beyond its earning capacity. For those who cannot afford to buy, tenancies are as scarce as National Lottery jackpot winners.

RESTRICTED ACCESS TO SEEDS

Seeds have become a packaged profit opportunity, especially seeds of genetically modified (GM) crops.

Monsanto, the world's leading supplier of GM seeds, controls nearly a quarter, 23%, of the global traded seeds market. Just nine more companies share a further 44%.[2] Monsanto is a US-based global corporation which made its name as an agrochemical company manufacturing products to oust the weeds and diseases that cut crop yields. Monsanto's global big seller was – is -- Roundup, a herbicide based on glyphosate, but patent protection expired in 2000. Monsanto needed a new big earner, preferably one that required customers to carry on buying Roundup. The processes of altering seeds, patenting the alterations, and selling the seeds for agriculture on a single-use licence, has immediate profit potential, and so Monsanto developed seeds resistant to Roundup, which could be applied to kill all weeds, leaving the crop unscathed.

Monsanto is not the only business with expertise in GMOs. Dow Agrosciences' 'Enlist' corn and soyabeans were ready for use in 2014, their special feature being resistance to the herbicide 2,4-D, which is made by many chemical companies and although the toxins it contains are suspected of causing human and animal diseases, its use is allowed on farms over most of the world, including Europe and the USA.

GM crops are, overwhelmingly, grown by agribusinesses for animal feed or fuel, not by small farmers for food. The 2014 edition of Friends of the Earth International's report *Who Benefits from GM Crops?* reported that:

- GM crops are grown on 12% of global arable land.
- The dominant GM crops are soya beans, maize (corn), oilseed rape (canola) and cotton.
- 92% of GM crops are grown in just six countries – USA, Brazil, Argentina, India, Canada and China. The first three

produce 77% of the world's GM crops, and the USA alone grows 40%.

- In 99% of GM plants, only one or two GM traits have been incorporated: herbicide tolerance and insect resistance. Weed and insect resistance to GM crops has become a serious problem.

For the first couple of years of cultivation, insect-resistant Bt[3] cotton would typically require fewer pesticides than its predecessor, but then insects started adapting to the toxins in the plants, and farmers were spending heavily on GM seed for what benefit? Agrochemical companies benefit from demand for pesticides, but farmers have to keep digging into their pockets. The same goes for herbicide-tolerance in GM crops such as maize, soya beans and oilseed rape. In Argentina, some 15 years of GM expansion have been accompanied by a twenty-fold explosion in agrochemical use.[4] The increase is enough to make one wonder if this is an important reason why agrochemical companies buy up seed companies – to create new markets for herbicides and pesticides. The companies are not having it all their own way. The Supreme Court in Brazil ruled in 2012 that Monsanto was wrong to charge farmers a 2% royalty on soya beans resistant to Monsanto's herbicide Roundup, because the patent protection for Roundup had expired. Farmers quickly launched claims for compensation running to about $1 billion.

Corporations selling GM seeds and agrochemicals naturally want their global markets to include the European Union, but eight European governments[5] allow no or minimal GM cultivation. The European Union Commission is not so hostile, and in February 2014 ministers representing a majority of the EU's population approved a GM maize called Pioneer 1507, bred to tolerate glufosinate herbicide and to be toxic to insect pests.

President George W Bush took a keen interest in the EU's resistance to GM, and in the mid '00s accused Europe of hindering "the great cause of ending hunger in Africa",[6] although he ignored the facts that most harvests of GM plants are destined to feed animals that will enter the food processing industry, or are processed for fuel, and are not for direct human consumption.

For many small farmers who planted GM seeds, the profits they hoped for proved illusory.[7] The seeds are more expensive than non-GM seeds, because of the licence fees remitted to the breeder; farmers are not allowed to save seed from one year's crop to the next, but have to buy a new batch; and the claimed yield increases have often not materialised. The 'desirable' traits are often formulated with the needs of the supplier and the agricultural processing industry uppermost, and have no relevance to the nutritional needs of hungry people, who after all lack power in the global economy.

The GM seeds companies like Monsanto have been able, without challenge, to commercialise such fundamental knowledge as genetic codes because there is no global political institution capable of limiting the activities of transnational corporations and their directors, whom the author Voldemar Tomusk, drawing on Leslie Sklair's global systems theory, called the "transnational capitalist class".[8]

In global systems theory, Leslie Sklair proposes the concept of an interlocking trio of global forces: transnational corporations, the elite transnational capitalist class, and the culture-ideology of consumerism. Voldemar Tomusk claims that the elite-based theory of globalisation did not go quite far enough because it gave insufficient importance to 'predatory capital',[9] the worldwide flow of capital searching out growth opportunities. Tomusk warned that predatory capital "turned the global economy into a ruthless war of everybody against everybody", just as the philosopher John Macmurray warned in these words written in 1949, criticising the concept of economic globalisation:

"A system of independent sovereign States in a world which is economically one society *cannot* achieve justice and must destroy freedom. For it is a system in which each government must attempt to control the economy of the whole world in the interest of its own citizens. So each industrial State tends to take on the character of a gigantic business combine in economic competition with all its rivals; and there is no common authority to hold the ring, and to formulate the rules of what is fair and what is foul play. Is it any wonder that such a situation leads to world wars, or that when they come there are no inhumanities to which the struggling adversaries will not stoop?"[10]

In the 65-plus years since Macmurray's analysis, there has been little to hinder transnational corporations in the pursuit of their economic ends, so even if there is no clear public wish for a small number of multinational corporations to control essentials such as the crop seeds on which global food supplies depend, there appears little that individuals can do about it.

SEEDS UNDER CORPORATE CONTROL

Massive business organisations dominate and overawe the world's small farmers. There are only a handful of global agrochemical giants. Syngenta is one, and its history illustrates the history of industrial power. The Syngenta story began in 1758 with the formation of Geigy in Basel, Switzerland. In 1970 Geigy merged with Ciba, founded in Basel in 1884. Ciba Geigy merged in 1982 with Sandoz, a German agrochemical company founded in 1876, and renamed itself Novartis. The Novartis group continued to grow, adding German company Merck & Co's crop protection business, for example, in 1997.

In the UK, the agrochemical company Zeneca was spun out of Imperial Chemical Industries (ICI) in 1994, and merged with Astra of Sweden in 1999 to form AstraZeneca. The following year, AstraZeneca[11] divested Zeneca Agrochemicals which merged with Novartis and the result was Syngenta.

Seed companies were acquired along the way. Ciba Geigy bought Funk Seeds International of the USA in 1974; the ICI offshoot Zeneca

Seeds merged with Cosun/Royal VanderHave Group to create Advanta in 1996. Eight years later Advanta was sold in two parts, one part to Syngenta and the other to Fox Paine, a California-based private equity investment company that also owned Seminis, the world's largest fruit and vegetable seeds company. Early in 2005, Fox Paine cashed in Seminis, selling it for $1.4 billion to --- Monsanto.

Six companies share the entire GM seed market, 76% of agrochemical sales, 75% of private-sector plant-breeding research and 60% of the global commercial seed market. Those companies are Monsanto, Dow Chemical and Du Pont (USA), Syngenta (Switzerland), and Bayer and BASF (Germany). Power indeed. Monsanto and Dow Chemical's Dow Agrosciences made a collaboration agreement in January 2006. The pact involved cross-licensing of intellectual property and of product licences in corn and soya beans, cross-licensing of cotton seed technologies, and settlement of outstanding legal disputes over the ownership of specific synthetic genes for cotton plants. Dow's property included Herculex™ and WideStrike™ insect-resistance traits, which the companies intended to combine with Monsanto's 'Roundup Ready' trait to create crops resistant to Roundup herbicide as well as with insect resistance. In 2007 Monsanto and Dow made an additional agreement to collaborate on SmartStax™ maize, containing eight different genes inserted for pest resistance and herbicide tolerance.

Monsanto and the US Government[12] jointly own the rights to 'terminator seeds', which produce plants with a gene to make seeds infertile, so farmers cannot save any for future use and must buy new supplies. Single-use seeds are produced with Genetic Use Restriction Technologies, or GURTs. Monsanto put its GURT programme on the shelf in 1999 as a result of political pressures, but it remains ready to be dusted down and pulled off, either as a commercial product or as a weapon of war. Seeds are essential to human food, and control over them gives control over human societies.

The downsides of GM seeds and seeds-chemicals linkages include higher costs for farmers, who are locked in to a purchasing portfolio. If they buy the seeds, but not the chemicals -- at present overwhelmingly the herbicide Round-up (glyphosate) -- which form the rest of the package, the crop will probably not thrive. When growers are committed to a suite of products, the suppliers can rack up the costs. What happens if plants are bred to be used with pesticides that turn out to be serious health hazards? What happens if new seed production fails? Farmers will not have their own saved seed to fall back on: corporations will be in control.

THE (IN)FAMOUS CASE OF PERCY SCHMEISER

Seed patents are power, and rights are zealously guarded. Monsanto gained a reputation for searching fields around GM crop sites to look for 'unlicensed' GM plants, and subsequently seeking recompense from the farmers concerned, even if the GM plants arrived uninvited, as a result of distribution methods beyond human control, such as the wind.

Percy Schmeiser, a farmer from Saskatchewan in Canada, planted a canola[13] crop in 1998. He used seed saved from the previous harvest, as was his practice. Unfortunately, his 1997 crop had been contaminated with GM canola patented by Monsanto. Mr Schmeiser said he did not know how the contamination occurred. It could have been from pollen carried by winds, birds, insects, or even humans. The wind may have blown GM seeds far from the fields where it was planted intentionally. Mr Schmeiser maintained that he did not want the GM seed on his land, but it got there anyway. Monsanto took him to court, for using seed without paying for a licence.

Thus began six years of difficulty for the Schmeiser family, entrapped within a prolonged legal process. In March 2001 a Canadian court ruled that Mr Schmeiser had planted seeds resistant to the herbicide Roundup without the correct licence from Monsanto, and that the origin of those seeds was irrelevant. In the judge's opinion, Mr Schmeiser should not have used the seed without paying Monsanto even if he had not wanted the seed on his farm in the first place, and it arrived by means that he could not control. Winds, birds and insects are not renowned for obeying farmers' orders. The court ordered Mr Schmeiser to pay around $Canadian 175,000 in costs and confiscated profits. He submitted an appeal, only to have it rejected by the Federal Court of Appeal in May 2002. He appealed again, to the Supreme Court of Canada, which gave its verdict in May 2004. The panel of nine judges ruled five to four in favour of Monsanto, but it was a qualified verdict and it saved Percy Schmeiser from financial ruin.

Five of the judges agreed that Mr Schmeiser had infringed Monsanto's patent, but the other four held that Monsanto did not have exclusive rights over the plants in which its patented genes had been found. The panel agreed to cancel both the order for Mr Schmeiser to forfeit his crop profits to Monsanto, and the order for him to pay all legal costs.

Despite this concession, the majority verdict by five of the judges gave Monsanto the signal that, in Canada at any rate, it could claim patent control over a crop grown from GM seed, even if the company 'owned' as little as one altered gene within the plant. Monsanto itself regarded the Supreme Court decision as a complete vindication of its business model, and on the Percy Schmeiser section of its website alleged that Mr Schmeiser "did not at all explain why he sprayed Roundup to isolate the Roundup Ready plants he found on his land; why he harvested the plants and segregated the seeds, saved them, and kept them for seed; why he planted them; and why, through his husbandry, he ended up with 1,030 acres of Roundup Ready canola which would have cost him $15,000".

Monsanto argues that Mr Schmeiser "is not a hero. He's simply a patent infringer who knows how to tell a good story. Unlike his neighbours, and the vast majority of farmers who plant patented seeds, Schmeiser saved seed that contained Monsanto's patented technology without a license".

Several other 'patent infringement' cases feature on the Monsanto website, part of the company's campaign to justify its seeds-agrochemicals packages. "Patents are necessary to ensure that we are paid for our products and for all the investments we put into developing these products," said a feature on the website headed 'Why does Monsanto sue farmers who save seeds?' On the basis that it is intent upon fairness for farmers, the company says that it invests $2.6 million a day to develop and bring new products to market, and that "it would be unfair to the farmers that honor their agreements to let others get away with getting it for free. Farming, like any other business, is competitive and farmers need a level playing field".

Thus Monsanto positions itself as the farmer's champion, patrolling the fields of the world to stamp out "seed piracy".[14] The unexpressed, taken-for-granted notions are that agribusiness exists to help farmers, and that farmers have a necessary and crucial partnership with agribusiness.

SIGNPOSTS?

Control over land and seeds conveys power, and increases the risks of small farmers being squeezed out of contention.

In addition, at some not-too-distant point in the future, the decline in fossil fuel availability will severely increase competition for energy supplies and/or decrease customers' capacity to afford energy. Multinational companies will stand more chance than individual farmers of securing the fuel and power that is available. The agribusiness, agrochemical and food industry sectors could well collaborate in an attempt to secure the lion's share of energy, and consequently intensify the flight of independent farmers from the land. This outcome would be high-risk for biodiversity, for food diversity and for soil fertility.

Over the longer term, possibly but by no means inevitably, the cost pressures resulting from scarcer and costlier fuels and raw materials, and from heavy levels of debt, might gradually erode corporate power, creating spaces in which small farms and rural businesses could flourish. This presupposes that there remain sufficient small-scale farmers, sufficiently resilient rural communities, to move into the new spaces.

---

[1] The rapprochement between the USA and Cuba, announced by presidents Barack Obama and Raul Castro in December 2014, may have beneficial economic repercussions if the US economic blockade is lifted, but that is not in President Obama's gift.

[2] Data from La Via Campesina, April 17th 2014.

[3] Bt is the bacterium Bacillus thuringiensis, which produces chemicals harmful to a range of insects.

[4] 'If we rely on corporate seed, we lose food sovereignty',
http://viacampesina.org/en/index.php/actions-and-events-mainmenu-26/world-social-forum-mainmenu-34/1394-tunis-2013-if-we-rely-on-corporate-seed-we-lose-food-sovereignty, March 31st 2013

[5] Austria, Bulgaria, Greece, Germany, Hungary, Italy, Luxembourg, Poland. European Commission, November 6th 2013.

[6] Quotation in 'Force feeding the world', media briefing from Friends of the Earth Europe, December 2005.

[7] In 'Warning shot', an article in the Soil Association's *Organic Farming*, spring 2010 pps. 24-27, Emma Hockridge and Isobel Tomlinson review 'The magnitude and impacts of the biotech and organic seed price premium' by Dr Charles Benbrook. Dr Benbrook found that by tying growers into seed purchasing agreements, agro-technology companies had been able to raise seed prices dramatically, compared with prices for non-GM and organic seeds, consequently cutting average incomes for GM crop producers. GM results in income transfer from farmers to agrotechnology corporations.

[8] Voldemar Tomusk's 'The rise of the transnational capitalist class and World Bank 'aid' for higher education' in *International Studies in Sociology of Education* 2002 vol.12 no.3 p336.

[9] Voldemar Tomusk, as above, p.339.

[10] In *Conditions of Freedom*, pps.42-43.

[11] AstraZeneca was in 2014 the subject of a hostile takeover bid by Pfizer of the USA. AstraZeneca rejected the approach.

[12] 'Terminator seeds' were developed by the Agricultural Research Service of the US Department of Agriculture and by a company called Delta & Pine Land. Monsanto agreed a takeover for Delta & Pine Land in 2006.

[13] Canola is known in the UK as oilseed rape.

[14] Term used in feature titled 'Pilot Grove Co-op', www.monsanto.com/newsviews/pages/pilot-grove-coop.aspx, accessed January 11th 2011.

CHAPTER 5
WAKE UP TO WANING OIL

CONFIDENCE ON CLOUD NINE

"The facts about our energy resources are sobering. The rapidity with which we are finding ways of spending that energy, often without realizing it, is shocking. The problems attendant in tapping unused reservoirs of energy are discouraging. Just the same, no one should say that man's standard of living is likely to toboggan for lack of energy – cheap energy. This optimism comes not from a blind faith in the scientist and engineer but, instead, from an infinite confidence, supported by a long record of the past, that man's ingenuity is equal to the task."

-- Charles A Scarlott, writing in *Man's Role in Changing the Face of the Earth*, published in 1956.[1]

This quotation from *Man's Role in Changing the Face of the Earth* reflects the supreme confidence in technology that characterises the human approach to intractable problems. Charles Scarlott was, at the time, manager of technical information services in the public relations department of the Stanford Research Institute, Menlo Park, California, and he was very well aware of rapidly rising energy use, even back in the 1950s, but he trusted the human mind to invent new, cheap and plentiful forms of energy, and policymakers by and large happily accepted this rosy vision.

The vision legitimised mining and drilling all around the globe.

Petroleum, gas and coal are organic products of past aeons.[2] Petroleum is a mix of hydrocarbons, oxygen, nitrogen, sulphur and other chemical elements, originally organic matter – phytoplankton and zooplankton – that has been transformed by bacteria, by heat and by pressure, over millions of years. Natural gas is predominately methane, mixed with ethane, butane and propane. Methane, CH_4, is a by-product of rotting vegetation. Butane and propane are more complex gases than methane, but like methane are alkanes, the 'paraffin' group of hydrocarbons. Coal, a solid hydrocarbon in gradations from lignite at 70% to 80% carbon to anthracite at over 90% carbon, is compressed ancient former living matter, typically large ferny plants.

Hydrocarbons drove the 20th century explosion in agricultural productivity. Natural gas is the chief feedstock for nitrogen fertiliser manufacture. Irrigation, pesticide production and mechanised cultivation are fuelled by oil. Lavish use of hydrocarbons gives the illusion of limitless potential growth in food production, an illusion that permeates all forms of economic activity.

Bizarre, unsustainable, energy-hungry developments include Ski Dubai, which opened in December 2005. Ski Dubai is a dome 85 metres high, covering 22,500 square metres, and has five slopes, the longest 400 metres with a 60-metre fall. The temperature inside is cooled to −1 to −2 degrees C (28 to 30 degrees F) all the time, when outside it may be over 50 degrees C (more than 120 degrees F). The dome, owned by the Majid Al Futtaim Group, is at the extreme end of energy-hungry leisure and tourism ventures, and may be a valid undertaking from the perspective of an individual company, but is more than dubious in the context of uncertain world energy supplies. Dubai, one of the seven United Arab Emirates on the Persian Gulf, itself has low oil reserves and borrowed heavily to reinvent itself as a global financial and tourism centre, a gamble that nearly came unstuck in 2008 when the world financial system nosedived, but fellow emirate nation Abu Dhabi offered emergency loans and construction continued, although at a slower pace. There are wondrous buildings planned for Dubai, where the world's tallest building, the Burj Khalifa, punctures the skyline, and carries the name of the ruler of Abu Dhabi in thanks for supplying the money to finish it. An architect called David Fisher planned an energy-generating revolving skyscraper called the Da Vinci Rotating Tower, but at the time of writing this remained a set of drawings, and Dubai's lavish buildings continued to guzzle energy.

EATING OIL

If the energy supplies to modern industrialised agriculture were cut off, tractors would stay inside their sheds, synthetic fertilisers would be a memory. Cows would go unmilked and crops unharvested, because machines long ago replaced agricultural workers. A precipitate return to energy solely from human-power and animal-power is unlikely, but unless energy consumption is curtailed and remaining farmland is protected, it will become impossible to feed the world.

The USA's profligate energy consumption results, directly and indirectly, in the loss of around three million acres of cropland a year. Two million acres are lost to water saturation, erosion and pollution. A million acres more succumb to roads, suburbs, shopping malls, and industrial developments.[3] Three million acres is 4,688 square miles, 0.13% of the whole land area of the United States, lost each year. That is an area three-fifths the size of Wales, or larger than the whole of Gambia or Jamaica.[4]

Energy applied to irrigation, in the form of powered pumps,[5] is siphoning aquifers dry. The Ogallala aquifer under about 174,000 square miles of the USA's Great Plans of the Mid West, from South Dakota to Texas, enables farming to prosper, but many parts of this underground fresh-water sea could be dry before 2030, according to economics and geography professor Kevin Mulligan.[6] Researchers at Utrecht University report that aquifer depletion is rapid in many of the world's principal farming regions, including the Mid West, the desert southern states, and the central valley of California in the USA; north-west India; and north-east China.[7]

By the mid 1990s, the food eaten by the typical American every year had devoured the equivalent of 400 gallons of oil[8] on the way to the plate or take-away carton. Food production in the USA uses up about 10 times more energy than is contained in the final product. Before the industrial revolution, farmers increased the productivity of plants and animals by selective breeding, and they spread animal waste in the form of farmyard manure, and composted plant residues, to improve the soil. Farming this way was labour-intensive. One person's direct labour might yield sufficient food to feed their family, but one person could not feed a village, let alone a small town -- until fossil fuels formed a temporary, one-time-only worker replacement force.

MONEY WELLS DRY UP

World oil consumption continues to edge upwards by 1%-1.5% annually.[9] The US Energy Information Administration (EIA) expects oil use in 2015 to grow by another 1.5% to 92.89 million barrels a day, 130,000 barrels less than daily production. Annual consumption would be pushing towards 34 billion barrels.

The EIA reckoned that in 2009 the world's proven reserves of crude oil totalled 1,342.2 billion barrels. That equalled 43.3 years' supply at the 2009 consumption rate. By 2013, reserves had inflated to 1,646.0 billion barrels, a phenomenal 22.6% growth in four years although no major new oilfields have been discovered. By 2013 the world appeared to have some 50 years of oil reserves. The inclusion of 'tight oil', which is 'liberated' by hydraulic fracturing, commonly called fracking, boosts the reserve figures but has a low return on the energy invested in extraction. The issue is not so much the absence of oil under the ground, but absence of money to give producers a profit sufficient to reinvest in exploration. The market is held back by impecunious consumers more than by dry wells. The actuary Gail Tverberg, who analyses energy and commodity prices, comes to this conclusion:[10]

> "Many people have the impression that falling oil prices mean that the cost of production is falling, and thus that the feared "peak oil" is far in the distance. This is not the correct interpretation, especially when many types of commodities are decreasing in price at the same time. *When prices are set in a world market, the big issue is*

affordability. Even if food, oil and coal are close to necessities, consumers can't pay more than they can *afford.*"

Oil with a high return on energy invested in extraction gives pricing flexibility. Where the energy return is small, the price needs to be consistently high, or there is no financial incentive to extract it.

Saudi Arabia, Venezuela and Canada are supposed to have the world's largest oil reserves. In both Venezuela and Canada, the energy gain from drilling 'oil' is low and in Canada is sometimes negative. The tar sands in northern Alberta are strip mined, and carried in trucks to processing plants where water is added to create a slurry, which is placed in separation vessels. The bitumen rises to the top. It is diluted with naphtha and further separated in centrifuges. The bitumen is processed again to yield gas oil, naphtha and hydrocarbon gases. The liquids are cleaned up with hydrogen to remove sulphur and nitrogen compounds. The naphtha is from local natural gas which is 'stranded' – i.e. there is not enough of it to justify exporting it through a long-distance pipeline. That limited supply of natural gas is an important element in the energy-heavy process to convert bitumen into synthetic crude oil.

The current financial cost of producing synthetic crude oil from sands is about $90 a barrel.[11] Ignoring the heavy environmental damage, the immediate production cost means that unless the oil is sold at over $100 a barrel, there is scant reason to produce it, and insufficient return to justify new investment. So is it realistic to assume that Canada will supply the world with over 173 billion barrels? Hardly. The oil price was on a plateau in 2011 and 2012, and in 2013 and 2014 trended downwards to below $100 a barrel, in September sinking close to $90. The fall continued in October and November, to under $80, followed by a precipitous collapse in late November and early December to under $63, and in January 2015 to below $50, for benchmark WTI (West Texas Intermediate).

Venezuela has a similar oil price threshold to surmount. Back in 2010 the EIA reckoned Venezuela had 99.4 billion barrels of oil reserves. By 2014 this total had multiplied to 297.7 billion barrels, because of the inclusion of extra-heavy oil which also costs around $90 a barrel to produce. In addition, carbon dioxide emissions from the extraction of heavy oil are about three times greater than from the production of light crude, and so do not help at all in the (muted) international efforts to row back the human contributions to climate change.

Converting Venezuelan heavy oil into usable crude needs natural gas, but there is not enough locally, so gas is imported from Colombia.

As for the fracking boom in the USA, it is supplying expensive oil, costing up to $100 and over per barrel to produce and causing environmental mayhem, including the consumption and pollution of large amounts of fresh water.

While there may be 50 years of oil left in theory – more if you include Arctic and deep-sea oil – much of it will remain where it is because too much energy will be needed to extract it, and in addition the pollution damage would be appalling. Are we down to 40 years? 30 years? We don't know, we can't know exactly, but it's fair to say we are the last oil generation.

VENEZUELA?

Venezuela's claimed reserves of 297.7 billion barrels of oil are the largest national total in the world but two-thirds of the reserves are extra-heavy oils which are expensive to extract and loss-making when the oil price is under $90 a barrel.

The slide in the oil price in the second half of 2014 and into 2015 was bad for the Venezuelan economy and could weaken popular support for the government. During the presidency of the late Hugo Chávez (1999-2013) and subsequently Nicolás Maduro, the Venezuelan state has forged a socialist agenda which includes supplying Cuba with some 42 million barrels of oil a year in return for 30,000 Cuban doctors working in Venezuela, a policy tailor-made to inflame anti-socialist and anti-Cuban prejudices in the USA.

Venezuela looks to China and Russia for capital investment, not to the USA. The daily total of Venezuelan oil exports to China is half a million barrels, some 60% of which is in repayment for loans of $36 billion issued to Venezuela by 2013.[12] May 2014 saw a deal between Venezuela and the Rosneft oil and gas company which is controlled by the Russian state. The Venezuelan state oil company, Petróleos de Venezuela (PDVSA), would receive $2 billion in advance for 7.5 million tons of oil products and just over 1.5 million tons of oil, over five years.[13]

Nicolás Maduro fears that the USA is behind the street protests which have disrupted government since Hugo Chávez died from an aggressive cancer in 2013. A more 'sympathetic' president with ties to the USA would divert oil and gas to North America rather than across oceans to China and Russia. According to *The Guardian*, Wikileaks revealed US cables about funding for opposition groups, and tactics to divide, isolate and penetrate the government.[14] The US House of Representatives, backing the Venezuelan opposition, passed a bill on May 28th 2014 to freeze the assets of government officials.[15] Their Venezuela Human Rights and Democracy Protection Act uses the language of 'democracy' to support opposition leader Henrique Capriles Radonski, who attended Columbia University and whose political movement has allegedly received several million dollars from US sources.[16]

Huge they are, but Venezuela's oil reserves are sufficient to last the world only a bare nine years at the 2014 rate of consumption.

SAUDI ARABIA?

Saudi Arabia has, apparently, nearly one-sixth of world oil reserves, 268.35 billion barrels of the 1,645.98 billion total.[17] Amazingly, despite thirty years of continuous pumping, and the absence of major oil finds, Saudi Arabia's reserves in 2009 were 60% higher than in 1980, and in 2014 2.3% more than in 2010. Similar inflation happened in other members of OPEC, the Organisation of Petroleum Exporting Countries,[18] in the late 1980s. The main reason for the inflation of reserves was OPEC's introduction of production quotas based on each member's stated oil reserves – so a logical if over-optimistic response was to 'find' new reserves.

No major fields have been discovered in Saudi Arabia since the 1960s, the last of any size being the Zuluf field in 1965, which started producing in 1973 and contained between 8.5 billion and 10 billion barrels. The Ghawar field, the largest in the world, was discovered in 1948, started production in 1951, and contained between 66 billion and 150 billion barrels.[19] The field had yielded some 72 billion barrels by summer 2014.[20] This means that the field is nearing exhaustion or, in the best case scenario, it is about half empty.

Saudi Aramco, the state oil company of Saudi Arabia, is typically secretive, and if the field is nearing depletion, would want to keep this information to itself for as long as possible. There are many signs, though, that the field is in the latter stages of its life. Water flooding, to fill the space created by the extraction of oil, is tried first and is regarded as the secondary stage of oil recovery: the remaining crude oil floats on the water and rises nearer to the surface. Water injection in the Ghawar field began as long ago as 1964.

Carbon dioxide injection is a technology of the final stages of oil recovery, when fields are near depletion. Aramco is injecting carbon dioxide into the Uthmaniyah section of the field, at the rate of 40 million cubic feet a day, to reduce the viscosity of the remaining oil so it can be recovered.[21] Aramco has been at pains to stress that the carbon dioxide injection programme is not because the oilfield is depleting, but to "quantify how much reserves we can recover and for the environment". So said Saad Turaiki, vice president of Aramco's southern area oil operations.[22]

Another sign that Saudi Arabia is past its oil peak was in 2010, when the *Saudi Gazette* reported, on November 10th, a speech by the late King Abdullah to Saudi students at universities in the United States. King Abdullah was explaining his decision to stop oil exploration in the kingdom, so that oil wealth would be saved and passed on to future generations. "Thank God, your homeland is proceeding resolutely to a prosperous future, God willing. And what is unknown is even better," the king told the students.[23]

The energy investment banker Matthew R Simmons, in his 2005 book *Twilight in the Desert: the Coming Saudi Oil Shock and the World Economy*, concluded that Saudi Arabia's fields were in decline, but his arguments were not universally accepted. Mr Simmons drowned in his hot tub, at home in Maine, in August 2010. Maine's Chief Medical Examiner, who noted that Mr Simmons, aged 67, suffered from heart disease, concluded that the death was accidental.[24]

CANADA?

Canada has the world's third largest reserves of crude oil according to the EIA. In 2009 those reserves were estimated at 178.09 billion barrels, or 13.3% of the global total, and in 2013 173.11 billion, 10.5% of a larger total inflated by higher reserve estimates for Venezuela.

As recently as 2003 Canada's oil reserves were stated as just 4.858 billion barrels. The oil sands of northern Alberta are the cause of the increase, regions of bituminous sands that can be processed, at high financial and environmental cost, into usable oil.

Richard Heinberg, in his web book *Searching for a Miracle: 'Net Energy' Limits and the Fate of Industrial Society*[25] explains the impact of Energy Return on Energy Invested, or EROEI. This ratio summarises the energy input required to obtain one unit of energy output. The world's largest oilfield, Saudi Arabia's Ghawar, has yielded an EROEI of 100 to 1, according to Heinberg's calculations. The global average EROEI for crude oil is some 19:1. As new oilfield discoveries wane, oil companies seek to drill in more challenging places, like the deep waters of the Gulf of Mexico, the Arctic shelf of Alaska, and northern Siberia. Very large amounts of energy are expended in securing oil from hostile and marginal environments. The oil sands of northern Alberta were regarded as marginal until the '00s. Their EROEI is between 5.2:1 and 5.8:1, Heinberg suggests.

That would still be a positive return, but after the 'easier' tar sands have been processed, the EROEI is likely to fall to marginal or negative levels.

As the energy demands of finding and extracting fossil fuels grow, the proportion of energy returned to the economy will fall. Put another way, the energy industries will themselves absorb escalating amounts of the energy extracted to power the world.

IRAN?

Iran is the country with the fourth largest oil reserves, data from the US Energy Information Administration shows. Reserves tend to jump independently of new discoveries. In 1980 Iran's reserves had been just 58.0 billion barrels. They leaped suddenly in 1988 to 92.85 billion barrels, not because any major new fields had been found, but because of OPEC's introduction of quotas based on reserves. Iran increased its notional reserves significantly again in 2004, with a jump to 125.80 billion barrels from 89.70 billion in 2003, the year when the USA led the invasion of Iraq, the western neighbour of Iran. In 2009 reserves had inflated to 136.15 billion barrels, just over 10% of the world total, and in 2014 157.30 billion barrels, about 9.5% of the estimated global total.

Iran's ageing oilfields need considerable investment in enhanced recovery technologies. Natural gas injection to raise the viscosity of remaining oil is an important aspect: the world's biggest gas injection scheme began in June 2009 on the Agha-Jari oilfield, a programme to inject 3.6 billion cubic feet, with the objective of increasing the field's daily output from 140,000 barrels to 200,000 barrels. Sanctions imposed by the USA have forced Iran to look outside the Western club for investment funds, which in large measure come from China.[26]

Western powers have tried to cut off supplies of capital and goods to Iran, allegedly to prevent development of a nuclear weapons programme, but another reason is to limit the modernisation of Iran's oil and gas infrastructure, thereby to slow flows of energy away from the West. US Treasury Secretary Jack

Low warned Russia in April 2014 that a $20 billion goods-for-oil barter deal with Iran could intensify Western sanctions against Russia, [27] over and above sanctions imposed after Russia's annexation of Crimea in March 2014.

IRAQ?
Iraq contains the fifth largest estimated oil reserves in the world. They have inflated voluminously since 1980, from 31.0 billion barrels then to 48.80 billion in 1987, 92.85 billion in 1988, 115.0 billion in 2009 and 140.30 billion in 2014![28]

These 'reserves' were opened up to international oil companies from 2008. BP, ExxonMobil, Shell, Total and ENI were among the successful bidders. Their success comes at a potentially explosive cost, because the withdrawal of US troops leaves the oilfields vulnerable to attack from Islamic State of Iraq and the Levant (ISIL) warriors and other zealots, nationalists, and rival powers directly or by proxy.

The contracts awarded in the first and second bidding rounds for Iraqi oil carried the expectation that production from the target fields would increase from 1.535 million barrels a day to 11.140 million by 2017, over seven times more. In fact, daily output rose between 2009 and 2013, but not by a multiple, only a fraction – just over a quarter, from 2.40 million barrels to 3.06 million. A further near quadrupling between 2013 and 2017 seems a fantasy forecast, given the dysfunctional geopolitical context.

Iraq, which also has the world's eighth largest natural gas reserves (and wastes a lot by flaring it off), sends a fifth of its lower-than-planned oil exports to Europe, almost a fifth to the USA, a similar quantity to India and just over an eighth to China. Exports are handicapped by pipeline damage and deterioration, and by insufficient storage at the principal port, Basra.

Two parallel pipelines run from Kirkuk in Iraqi Kurdistan to Ceyhan in Turkey, but both have damaged sections, and even if they were kept in repair and able to flow at capacity, oil to fill them would have to come from southern Iraq through the Strategic

Pipeline, which is itself deteriorated and disrupted. Another pipeline, from Kirkuk to Banias on Syria's Mediterranean coast, is closed, as is a pipeline into Saudia Arabia. ISIL forces were straining to take Kirkuk in the latter months of 2014, after seizing Mosul, Baiji and Tikrit in June.

The pretence that the 2003 invasion of Iraq by the 'Coalition of the Willing' was not an 'oil war' was all but over within a couple of years. Article 109 of the country's post-Saddam written constitution[29] created the framework for oil companies to siphon off Iraq's energy wealth. Article 109 stated:

First: The federal government with the producing governorates and regional governments shall undertake the management of oil and gas extracted from current fields provided that it distributes oil and gas revenues in a fair manner in proportion to the population distribution in all parts of the country with a set allotment for a set time for the damaged regions that were unjustly deprived by the former regime [Saddam Hussein] and the regions that were damaged later on, and in a way that assures balanced development in different areas of the country, and this will be regulated by law.

Second: The federal government with the producing regional and governorate governments shall together formulate the necessary strategic policies to develop the oil and gas wealth in a way that achieves the highest benefit to the Iraqi people using the most advanced techniques of the market principles and encourages investment *(sic)*."

The 'market principles' most popular in Iraq's government, in relation to the oilfields, were Production Sharing Agreements. The nominal ownership of the oilfields remains in the state's hands, but companies which make sharing agreements can, under current accounting conventions, log the oil reserves in their own accounts.[30]

Production Sharing Agreements last, typically, from 25 to 40 years, and a government's share of costs and revenues is fixed at the outset of the contract. The problem is not the concept of the

Production Sharing Agreement, but its application. Agreements are rarely in the public domain because of commercial confidentiality, and so the revenues flowing to oil companies cannot be scrutinised publicly.

The intended fate of the oilfields was decided well in advance of the start of the second Iraq War[31] in 2003. The 'Future of Iraq' project, initiated by the US State Department, was in motion by April 2002. The project included 17 working groups, each including 'experts' chosen by the State Department, and Iraqi exiles ill-disposed to Saddam Hussein. The groups met in Washington and London.[32] The working group for oil recommended that Production Sharing Agreements should be the way ahead for Iraqi oil, once Saddam was deposed. US and UK oil companies, notably ExxonMobil, Chevron Texaco, BP, and the Anglo-Dutch group Shell, were expected to benefit handsomely. Estimates in PLATFORM's 2005 report, *Crude Designs: the rip-off of Iraq's oil wealth*,[33] suggest that a sum between US\$74 billion and \$194 billion, over the life of the agreements, could go to oil companies instead of to the people of Iraq. These estimates were based on an oil price of just \$40 a barrel, but in May 2014 the price for West Texas Intermediate exceeded \$104[34] a barrel, and Brent crude was over \$110. The one-year forecast was for \$120. The higher the price, the greater the financial flows to the oil companies, compared with revenue to the government, because of the way the agreements were constructed. The 40% to 45% falls in oil prices between May and December 2014 have a major downside in that oil companies are less able to make major repairs or to undertake capital investment.

Iraq is a disaster, and in so far as there were any plans for after the 'coalition's' invasion, they failed. Many in the Pentagon had favoured former exile Ahmed Chalabi as 'their man' in charge of oil within the Iraqi government, but Iraq's voters showed no great gratitude to the Americans and British who removed Saddam Hussein. The national elections on December 15th 2005 yielded not one seat for Chalabi or his party, the USA-backed Iraqi National Congress. The elections were a victory for the United Iraq Alliance, a coalition of Shia Moslem groups, which secured 128 of the 275 seats. The Kurdish parties from northern Iraq gained 53 seats, and the parties dominated by Sunni Moslems, 44 seats. A permanent government was not agreed until May 2006, and the fearsome violence within Iraq prevented the new administration from governing effectively. Western oil companies lost ground in the oilfield exploration and development auctions in 2009. Only one winning bid was led by a US company – Exxon Mobil – and only one, Occidental Petroleum, was a minor partner in a winning bid, according to an analysis by Jim Jubak.[35] The winning companies included Gazprom and Lukoil of Russia, CNPC of China, Sonangol of Angola, and TPAO of Turkey.

Elections in March 2010 failed to improve national security or cohesiveness, or to stop the inter-regional arguments over control of (and revenue from) oil exports.[36] Many potential candidates were prohibited from standing because of their previous political affiliations, and prolonged bickering after the vote meant that a new government was not in place until November 2010. New elections on April 30th 2014 returned outgoing prime minister Nouri al-Maliki as leader of the largest group, but formation of a new government took months until Haider al-Abadi became prime minister in September 2014. Both Haider al-Abadi and his predecessor Nouri al-Maliki are Shia Muslims, while ISIL fighters are Sunni (like the late, executed Saddam Hussein). The continuing, endemic violence within Iraq is not conducive to stable government, infrastructure improvements, or confidence in the future.

USA?

The USA's much-publicised 'energy revival', dependent on hydraulic fracturing – fracking -- of oil-bearing shale rocks, has been over-magnified, yielding mainly debts and serious pollution. Yes, USA has increased oil production from 9.13 million barrels a day in 2009 to 12.32 million in 2013, and has trimmed consumption from 19.50 million barrels a day in 2008 to 18.49 million in 2012, but that still leaves a large gap of over 6.17 million barrels a day, 2.25 billion barrels a year.

The manufacture of usable oil from shales, fine-grained sedimentary rocks with high levels of organic matter, results in serious environmental harm such as carbon dioxide emissions to groundwater and surface water pollution, as well as returning a low EROEI ratio, in the range 1.5:1 to 4:1, according to Richard Heinberg.[37] Yet the dirty technology of shale oil extraction is becoming accepted by governments around the world, including in China and Brazil.[38]

Frackers are running out of cash. Bloomberg News analysed 61 fracking companies in 2014 and found that their debts had nearly doubled in four years, but their revenues rose just 5.6%. Possibly, if the crude oil price rose to $150 a barrel or more, some frackers would be able to repay their loans a little more easily, but an oil price at least 50% higher than the level current in September 2014 would slash demand and force societies to adopt less energy-intensive economies. The sliding oil price in the closing months of 2014 and into 2015 made fracking even less viable economically.

Bloomberg found that the 61 companies had debts of $164.6 billion by the first quarter of 2014. In several, interest payments ate over 20% of revenues. At one, Quicksilver, interest payments almost reached 45% of revenue.

"Drillers are caught in a bind," said Bloomberg. "They must keep borrowing to pay for exploration needed to offset the steep production declines typical of shale wells.

"For companies that can't afford to keep drilling, less oil coming out means less money coming in, accelerating the financial tailspin."[39]

If easier oil were to be found, no one would be fracking.

But the easy oil has gone.

IT'S ALL ABOUT THE ENERGY RETURN ON ENERGY INVESTED

The five countries of Venezuela, Saudi Arabia, Canada, Iran and Iraq account for over 60% of the world's estimated oil reserves. For Saudi Arabia the issue is depletion. Iran has troubles of depletion, weak infrastructure and little capital. In Iraq, probable over-statement is accompanied by the absence of stable government and the presence of violence, not least the statehood ambitions of ISIL. Iraq, Iran and Saudi Arabia are vulnerable to doctrinal skirmishes and schisms. In the case of Canada and Venezuela, the main issues are the energy and environmental costs of extracting and processing bitumen sands into oil.

How much oil is it practicable to extract from our heavily mined planet? We need to remove from the stated reserve figures the unexplained rises recorded by OPEC members especially in the late 1980s, and we should also reduce the apparent oil sands reserves, and the shale oil, because not all will yield an energy gain.

Gail Tverberg, an actuary in the USA, studies the implications for the economy of the rising extraction costs of oil and other non-renewable resources. She writes:

> "When production costs are higher, someone loses out. It is as if the economy is becoming less and less efficient. It takes more people, more energy products, and more equipment to produce the same amount of oil. This leaves fewer people and less energy products to produce the goods and services that people really want, putting a squeeze on the economy. The economy tends to grow less quickly because part of the goods and services available are being channelled into less productive operations.

> "The situation of the economy becoming less and less efficient at producing oil is called *diminishing returns*. A similar problem exists with fresh water in many parts of the world. We can extract more fresh water, but it takes deeper wells. Or we have to ship in water from a

distance, using a pipeline or trucks. Or we need to use desalination. Water is still available but at a higher per-gallon price."

-- 'Oil limits and the economy: one story, not two', www.ourfiniteworld.com, March 21st 2014

So even if oil is in the ground, and even if extraction will yield a positive energy return (a less and less likely possibility as the easiest deposits are consumed) before long drilling may not yield a financial return.

Major oil companies like Shell and Chevron have programmes to convert natural gas into liquid fuels. Shell and Qatar Petroleum have a huge investment – the plant cost about $19 billion -- to convert natural gas into fuel liquids at the Pearl plant in Qatar. The Pearl plant has a planned life of 55 to 60 years, during which time it would have produced some 3 billion barrels of liquid fuels.[40] This is not an efficient use of gas, because about 40% of its energy is lost in the process, and emissions of CO_2 are 20% to 25% greater than from the production of conventional liquid fuels.[41]

The Pearl venture illustrates the unpalatable truth about the remaining quantities of extractable crude oil: the investment in the plant is so huge, and the energy return on energy invested (EROEI) so low, that it would not have been constructed if supplies of conventional oil were sufficient for future needs. Typical EROEI for gas-to-liquids is probably about 3:1, lower than for oil from the more accessible of the exploited tar sands. If there are accidents, the energy costs of cleaning up after accidents further erode the EROIE.[42]

Leaving aside the higher risk of accidents and pollution in difficult environments, such events as the Deepwater Horizon explosion and well burst in the Gulf of Mexico in 2010, which killed 11 workers and untold wildlife, the world's increasing reliance on fuels manufactured using energy-intensive processes means that proportionately less fuel will be available for all other uses.

Overdosing on Gas

The USA, with 4.4% of the world's population, is the world's major gas guzzler, consuming over 21% of the world's annual total, a marginally higher proportion than the 20.7% of world oil which the USA also swallows. There is nowhere near enough gas for the world to consume at anything like the same rate as the USA. Even though the numbers sound enormous – reserves of 6,845.57 trillion cubic feet in 2013, according to the EIA – at current consumption rates that is enough for 57 years, if all could be used. This horizon would roll closer, quickly, if the gas-to-liquids industry became a major user of the raw energy, and in Qatar that is happening. Ideally consumption would be falling, but the opposite is the case, an increase of 10% between 2008 and 2012.

The Earth's gas powerhouses are Russia, Iran and Qatar, with estimated reserves of 1,688 trillion, 1,193 trillion and 885.29 trillion cubic feet. Saudi Arabia's 290.81 trillion cubic feet are a distant fourth. These four countries contain just on 60% of the estimated world gas reserves.[43]

The importance of political stability in the Middle East and Eurasia to world gas supplies cannot be overstated. Currently Iran is flaring off gas because Western sanctions have impeded development of the infrastructure to make use of it. The sanctions are causing the world to run out of gas sooner than need be.

China's strenuous efforts to acquire gas include joint ventures with the National Iranian Oil Company, although the relations are not always harmonious. In April 2014 the Iranian government terminated China National Petroleum Corporation's contract to develop the Azadegan oilfield,[44] apparently out of frustration at lack of progress. Meanwhile Russia, the top nation for gas reserves, is exporting gas to China from eastern Siberia.

Modern agriculture, so dependent on oil, also consumes natural gas, which is the principal feedstock for large-scale ammonia production by the Haber process. Around 80% of the world's ammonia production is used for the manufacture of nitrogen fertiliser,[45] a critical link in the oil- and gas-saturated business that is modern agriculture.

Farming's reliance on oil and gas, and the long and often complex supply chains from farm to plate, are colossal handicaps in the new age of energy vulnerability. Food will be scarcer and costlier, and like oil will be vulnerable to smash-and-grab wars, which accomplish little but pointless destruction and the ignition of new wars.

FLASHPOINTS IN CENTRAL ASIA

The chess game of geopolitical strategy is aggressive around the Caspian Basin oil and gas fields of the former Soviet Union in Central Asia.

The country of Kazakhstan typifies the attractions and problems of Central Asia. Kazakhstan, which in 2014 had a population of about 16.8 million, was a republic of the Soviet Union until declaring independence in 1991, and Russia retains 6,000 square kilometres of the Baykonur Cosmodrome on lease until 2050. There is a religious divide, with rather more Moslems than Russian Orthodox Christians.

Kazakhstan has become an elective dictatorship: President Nursultan A Nazarbayev, first elected in December 1991, was re-elected with a reported 91.5% of the vote for a further seven years in December 2005, and in 2007 succeeded in changing the national constitution to remove term limits on his presidency, and to give him and his family immunity from prosecution for acts committed during his rule. His bank accounts became an official state secret as a result of these constitutional changes.[46]

President Nazarbayev was re-elected in 2011. He appoints ministers and makes the big decisions. His family and appointees control the economy including oil and gas, uranium and the national media. Opposition to Nazarbayev's rule has been muted, partly because of the opportunities of rapid economic growth, but also because of repression.[47]

Kazakhstan has large uranium reserves, about 12% of the world total, and in 2013 was responsible for 38% of global uranium output. Of the 17 uranium mines, five are fully owned by the state company Kazatomprom, and the other 12 are joint ventures with partners from nations east and west, including Russia, China and France.[48] Uranium is not all: Kazakhstan has, in addition to oil and gas, reserves of coal, iron ore, chromium, copper, zinc, silver, gold, and other vital components of industrial technology.

The US military has access to the airport at the southern Kazakh city of Almaty. In 2004 the US announced that it was helping Kazakhstan to build a military base to protect the oilfields in the west of the country, and said that joint military training exercises would continue in the future. NATO, the North Atlantic Treaty Organisation, signed a liaison agreement with Kazakhstan in October 2005, to try and counterbalance the July 2005 decision of Kazakhstan's southern neighbour, Uzbekistan, to order the US military to vacate its airbase at Karshi-Khanabad within 180 days.

Western companies have significant investments in Kazakh oil fields to protect. Chevron is the most heavily committed, with a 50% stake in the world's deepest-operating super giant oilfield, Tengiz, producing some 540,000 barrels a day from depths exceeding 12,000 feet. Chevron also owns 18% of the Karachaganak field, second only to Tengiz in Kazakh production.[49] Other oil majors in the country include Conoco Phillips, ENI, ExxonMobil, Shell and Total from the USA and Europe, Lukoil from Russia, and China National Petroleum Corporation (CNPC) and PetroChina from China. In 2005 CNPC bought Petrokazakhstan – based in the oil sands zone of Alberta, Canada – for £2.4 billion. As part of the deal, the Kazakh government (over which the Nazarbayev family has such a hold) received a holding of 33%.[50] A pipeline to carry Kazakh oil to China came into use in December 2005, going in the opposite direction to an earlier pipeline, opened in 2001, which takes Kazakh oil west to the Black Sea. In 2009 China lent $10 billion to aid the development of Kazakhstan, Kyrgyzstan and Tajikistan, and gained a half of the

Kazakh oil company MangistauMunaiGas in a joint deal with KazMunaiGas, owned by the state of Kazakhstan.

Oil production hit a barrier in 2013 when development of the Kashagan oilfield in the Caspian Sea, a project costing some $48 billion, was halted because of serious defects in pipes carrying sulphurous natural gas from the field. The closedown removed 2.4 million tons from the national estimate of 83 million tons of oil for 2014.[51]

The USA's worldwide net of military bases signal determination to retain access to energy supplies, although counter-alliances to contain the USA are developing fast. In Central Asia, Uzbekistan prefers to co-operate with Russia. Turkmenistan, important to the US because of its location immediately to the north of Iran, refused to allow the American military to build a military base but agreed in 2010 to allow NATO to transport various cargoes, but not arms, through its territory. Kyrgyzstan, lying between China and Kazakhstan, hosts Russian and US military bases, and is itself a candidate for schism. A pro-democracy coup in April 2010 ousted the president, Kurmanbek Bakiyev. Elections in 2011 returned Almazbek Atambayev as president. His administration told the US military to vacate their Manas air base near the capital, Bishkek, before the start of July 2014. Manas was an important staging post for supplies and personnel entering and exiting Afghanistan, but on June 3rd 2014 the US handed the base over to the Kyrgyzstan state.

The Shanghai Cooperation Organisation – the Asian countries of China, Russia, Kazakhstan, Kyrgyzstan, Tajikistan and Uzbekistan – in July 2005 asked the USA to give a timetable for withdrawal from its many bases in the region, not a popular suggestion with the US Military. Russia and China held their first joint military exercises in August 2005, and signed a military co-operation protocol in November 2010.

Competition for access to oil and other key resources becomes more intense year on year. The US administration was so desperate for oil companies to find new fields that the 2005 Energy Policy Act authorised $8 billion in subsidies to energy businesses. That was $25 for every one of the USA's 297.56 million inhabitants[52] – money that many of their representatives believed would be better used to improve energy efficiency in homes, businesses and transport. The act pushed renewable energy to the sidelines, and channelled financial support to fossil fuels.[53] It provided a lot of money for nuclear power, including indemnities of $2 billion for liabilities resulting from the construction of up to six new nuclear power plants, and $1.25 billion in federal funds for a nuclear plant to produce electricity and hydrogen. The Price-Anderson Nuclear Industries Indemnity Act, which limits the liability insurance obligations for the nuclear power industry, was extended to 2025, and employees and contractors at nuclear installations are allowed to carry guns.

Opposition within the USA to the pro-oil, pro-nuclear thrust of the Energy Policy Act was fierce, vocal and widespread, yet still ineffective. Congressman Jay Inslee, a Democrat from Washington state, commented:[54]

"There is a sad irony in the fact that humans are now relying on energy from fossilized dinosaurs and vegetation, which died most likely as a result of climate change, to such a great extent that we are altering the nature of our own atmosphere."

Optimistic utterances about nuclear power were muted after the serious leaks of radioactivity from the Fukushima Daiichi nuclear plant north of Tokyo, following the disastrous earthquake and tsunami in March 2011. All of a sudden, the very real dangers of nuclear power were all too obvious. The prospect of nuclear energy filling some of the gap caused by declining oil began to seem unlikely. Yet official nervousness about electricity shortages is not in abeyance for long, and in November 2014 there were media reports[55] that Yuichiro Ito, governor of Kagoshima province in the south of Kyushu island, had just authorised the restarting of two reactors at Sendai power station, despite considerable public opposition.

Even if there are no nuclear disasters in the near future, and nuclear-fuelled generation of electricity increases, electricity is only one form of energy, and on its own is insufficient for modern agriculture, for example, to continue. Intensive agriculture needs energy in many other forms too. Without oil for fuels and lubricants, and for manufacturing the myriads of products used in farming and food production, and without natural gas for manufacturing nitrogen fertilisers, commercial agriculture as we know it could not function. Without intensive large-scale agriculture, supermarkets' just-in-time supply chains could not work, and without oil there could not be long supply chains.

And we are running out of easily drilled oil.

DEADWEIGHT OF DEBT

For how long can the USA continue to consume over a fifth of the oil and gas produced on earth? No more than one generation for oil and two for gas – that's what the reserves tell us – but events in the real world are very likely to complicate the picture. Much depends on the length of time the USA can continue to pay interest on its mega debts. The federal national debt was expected to reach $17,900 billion -- $17.9 trillion – by the end of 2014. Debt accumulation continued in 2015, and by March 30th the federal debt was nudging $18.2 trillion. Federal debt is only 30% of the total: the rest is state and local government debt, bank and financial institution debt, business debt and household debt. The total of almost $61.4 trillion was equivalent to more than $700,000 per family group, while average savings per family were under $7,800.[56]

Debts this great would probably take between one and two centuries to repay even if no new debt was incurred, households earned enough to pay taxes, the government used revenues to repay debt, and individuals had enough post-tax income to repay their own debts. All this debt repayment would take dangerous bites out of the consumer spending on which 'economic growth' has depended, making the growth impossible. Impasse!

Only by maintaining the dollar as the world's reserve currency, and by using that financial power to keep interest rates low, can the US afford interest payments on the debt. To maintain economic clout, the US administration believes it must control the globe – and space – with military might. Defence spending in 2013 was $640 billion,[57] more than the eight next biggest spenders combined.

$640 billion is nearly $5,500 per US household, per year, spent to retain US military 'advantage', money that Americans cannot afford, money that could be better spent creating a balanced low-energy economy.

What happens if the USA defaults? Military solutions to stop creditors in their tracks? Bio warfare? With over 1,000 bases in 63 countries – or more, the real numbers are not in the public domain – the US's global military network is energy-hungry, and without the energy, could not exist.

The trend to use drones instead of people is one way to try and maintain control at lower cost. No one, no matter how wealthy or well protected, is safe from a drone attack by almost anyone. Controlling drone use could easily become as problematic as controlling gun ownership, and could herald further dangerous military fragmentation, of which ISIL is an early warning.

A more dangerous world is not conducive to the repayment of debt.

---

[1] Charles A Scarlott, writing in *Man's Role in Changing the Face of the Earth* (p.1021), edited by William L Thomas Jr and published by the University of Chicago Press in 1956.

[2] Some scientists suggest that inorganic oil also exists in large quantities, but hypotheses are at an early stage. See Chapter 6, 'Energy Questions but Few Answers'.

[3] Figures from' Food, land, population and the US economy', by David Pimental and Mario Giampietro. Carrying Capacity Network, November 21st 1994. Quoted by Dale Allen Pfeiffer in *Eating Fossil Fuels*, From The Wilderness Publications, 2003.

[4] These figures for land loss are corroborated by the University of Tennessee and the Sun Grant Initiative, http://bioweb.sungrant.org. In 'Land base', updated on 10th June 2008, Marie Walsh wrote that between 1997 and 2002 3% of the USA's cropland, 14 million acres, were lost from crop production.

[5] Solar-powered irrigation pumps are a promising development from an energy point of view, although they do not change the rate of water depletion.

[6] Dr Mulligan, of Texas Tech, is quoted in 'New west, new dustbowl' by Courtney White, http://newwest.net/topic/article/new_west_new_dust_bowl/C35/L35/, April 28th 2010.

[7] The Utrecht study, led by Marc Bierkens, is reported in 'Groundwater depletion rate accelerating worldwide', release from the American Geophysical Union, September 23rd 2010.

[8] Figure from 'Food, land, population and the US economy', by David Pimental and Mario Giampietro. Carrying Capacity Network, November 21st 1994. Quoted by Dale Allen Pfeiffer in *Eating Fossil Fuels*, From The Wilderness Publications, 2003.

[9] US Energy Information Administration, Short-Term Energy Outlook, September 9th 2014.

[10] 'Low oil prices: sign of a debt bubble collapse, leading to the end of oil supply?' by Gail Tverberg, http://ourfiniteworld.com/2014/09/21/low-oil-prices-sign-of-a-debt-bubble-collapse-leading-to-the-end-of-oil-supply/, September 21st 2014.

[11] 'Peak Oil becomes an issue again after the IEA revised its predictions' by Tom Dispatch, http://oilprice.com/Energy/Crude-Oil/Peak-Oil-becomes-an-Issue-Again-after-the-IEA-Revised-its-Predictions.html, January 9th 2014.

[12] 'China's paying Venezuela to stay afloat', by Patricia Rey Mallén, www.ibtimes.com/chinas-paying-venezuela-stay-afloat-now-maduro-wants-be-friends-1572022, April 15th 2014.

[13] 'Rosneft buying $2 billion oil as Venezuela seeks funding' by Jose Orozco and Pietro D Pitts, www.bloomberg.com/news/2014-05-26/pdvsa-rosneft-sign-2b-oil-deal-amid-financial-crunch.html, May 26th 2014.

[14] 'Venezuela protests are sign that US wants our oil, says Nicolás Maduro' by Seumas Milne and Jonathan Watts, www.theguardian.com/world/2014/apr/08/venezuela-protests-sign-us-wants-oil-says-nicolas-maduro, April 8th 2014.

[15] 'House passes sanctions bill over Venezuelan opposition's concerns', Think Progress, http://thinkprogress.org/world/2014/05/28/3441870/sanctions-bill-venezuela/, May 28th 2014.

[16] 'Venezuela: did opposition presidential candidate Henrique Capriles have a falling out with his US handlers?' by John Robles, www.globalresearch.ca/venezuela-did-opposition-presidential-candidate-henrique-capriles-have-a-falling-out-with-his-us-handlers/5326982, March 15th 2013.

[17] Energy Information Administration. World reserves for 2013, Saudi reserves for 2014.

[18] There are 12 members of OPEC: Algeria, Angola, Ecuador, Iran, Iraq, Kuwait, Libya, Nigeria, Qatar, Saudi Arabia, United Arab Emirates and Venezuela.

[19] Saudi Arabia oilfield data from 'Saudi Arabia: an attempt to link oil discoveries, proven reserves and production data' by Sam Foucher, www.theoildrum.com/node/2945, January 3rd 2008. The paper includes oilfield estimates from Petroconsultants, Colin Campbell, Matthew Simmons, Fredrik Robelius and others.

[20] 'Aramco pride at 'pampered' Ghawar'', www.upstreamonline.com/live/article1238371.ece, April 8th 2010. Output since 2010 calculated from daily average of 5 million barrels a day.

[21] 'Aramco pride at 'pampered' Ghawar'', op.cit.

[22] Reported in 'Aramco pride at 'pampered' Ghawar'', op.cit.

[23] 'New oil fields saved for future generations: King', www.saudigazette.com.sa/index.cfm?method=home.regcon&contentID=2010070377026, July 3rd 2010.

[24] 'Matthew Simmons, who said global crude production has peaked, dies at 67', by Edward Klump and David Wethe, www.bloomberg.com/news/2010-08-09/matthew-simmons-investment-banker-peak-oil-theory-advocate-dies-at-67.html, August 9th 2010.

[25] Available on http://richardheinberg.com, dated November 12th 2009.

[26] Iran profile from the US Energy Information Administration, accessed November 10th 2010. www.eia.doe.gov/countries/country-data.cfm?fips=IR.

[27] 'US warns Russia over any oil-for-goods deal with Iran', http://uk.reuters.com/article/2014/04/10/us-usa-russia-iran-idUSBREA391Y920140410, April 10th 2014.

[28] Iraq profile from the US Energy Information Administration, accessed November 10th 2010, www.eia.doe.gov/countries/country-data.cfm?fips=IZ. 2014 figure from EIA data on national oil reserves.

[29] The constitution was on the BBC website at http://news.bbc.co.uk/1/shared/bsp/hi/pdfs/24_05_05.constit.pdf in 2006 but was later removed. In 2014 it could be accessed via Wikipedia, 'Constitution of Iraq'.

[30] *Crude Designs: The Rip-off of Iraq's Oil Wealth*, from PLATFORM, November 2005. PLATFORM assesses the impact of British oil corporations on development, environment and human rights. *Crude Designs* was co-published by the Global Policy Forum, Institute for Policy Studies, Oil Change International, New Economics Foundation, and War on Want.

[31] The Gulf War of 1990-1991 is also known as the First Iraq War, the Kuwait War, Operation Desert Shield and Operation Desert Storm, and other permutations.

[32] 'From Washington to Baghdad: planning Iraq's oil future', p.16 in *Crude Designs*, published by PLATFORM, see above.

[33] The report could in December 2014 be viewed on www.carbonweb.org in the Iraq section.

[34] 2014 data from www.oil-price.net accessed May 27th 2014.

[35] 'How Iraq is squeezing out Big Oil' by Jim Jubak, http://articles.moneycentral.msncom/Investing/JubaksJournal/how-iraq-is-punishing-... , December 17th 2009.

[36] See 'Iraq agrees to pay companies pumping Kurdish oil, exports to resume Feb 1', www.bloomberg.com/news/2011-01-23/iraq-to-pay-companies-pumping-oil-in-kurdish-zone-exports-to-start-feb-1.html, January 23rd 2011.

[37] 'Searching for a Miracle: 'Net Energy' Limits and the Fate of Industrial Society', http://richardheinberg.com/searching-for-a-miracle, November 12th 2009.

[38] 'Oil shale economics', Wikpedia, updated 9th October 2010, accessed November 12th 2010.

[39] 'Shakeout threatens shale patch as frackers go for broke' by Asjylyn Loder, www.bloomberg.com/news/2014-05-26/shakeout-threatens-shale-patch-as-frackers-go-for-broke.html, May 27th 2014.

[40] 'Qatar's Pearl GTL plant set for 2012 completion', http://ameinfo.com/blog/energy-oil-and-gas/qatars-pearl-gtl-plant-set-for-completion/, September 28th 2010.

[41] 'Can Qatar's success with gas-to-liquids fuels be repeated in the US?', http://oilprice.com/Energy/Natural-Gas/Can-Qatars-Success-with-Gas-to-Liquids-Fuels-Be-Repeated-in-the-U.S.html, March 10th 2013.

[42] Robert L Hirsch, senior energy advisor at Management Information Services Inc, included a useful chart in his presentation 'Elements of the World's Energy Future', dated May 12th 2008.

[43] Data from the Energy Information Administration, accessed May 28th 2014.

[44] 'China aims to boost military relations with Iran', www.reuters.com/article/2014/05/05/us-china-iran-idUSBREA4407A20140505, May 5th 2014.

[45] Figure from the International Fertilizer Industry Association.

[46] 'Kazakh president to run for office in 2012', by Richard Orange, www.telegraph.co.uk/news/worldnews/asia/kazakhstan/8006821/Kazakh-president-to-run-for-office-in-2012.html, September 16th 2010.

[47] 'Kazakhstan prisoners protest by self-mutilation', by Pavol Stracansky, www.ipsnews.net/2010/10/kazakhstan-prisoners-protest-by-self-mutilation/, October 10th 2010.

[48] 'Uranium and nuclear power in Kazakhstan', World Nuclear Association, www.world-nuclear.org/info/Country-Profiles/Countries-G-N/Kazakhstan/, April 2014 version.

[49] Data from the EIA, dated October 28th 2013.

[50] Data in this paragraph on Kazakh oilfields relate to 2014.

[51] 'Kashagan halt leads Kazakhstan to cut 2014 oil output forecast' by Nariman Gizitdinov, www.bloomberg.com/news/2014-05-28/kashagan-halt-leads-kazakhstan-to-cut-2014-oil-output-forecast.html, May 28th 2014.

[52] Figure from US Census Bureau, at November 1st 2005.

[53] The online encyclopaedia Wikipedia has a clear summary of the Energy Policy Act at http://en.wikipedia.org/wiki/Energy_Policy_Act_of_2005

[54] Jay Inslee was commenting for the Apollo Alliance, representing the Union of Concerned Scientists, the Sierra Club, League of Conservation Voters, Greenpeace, and many labour unions in the United States. 'The new Apollo energy project', May 18th 2005.

[55] 'Japan edges back towards nuclear power with vote to restart reactors' by Justin McCurry, The Guardian, October 28th 2014, www.theguardian.com/world/2014/oct/28/japan-nuclear-power-reactors-satsumasendai-fukushima

[56] Figures from www.usdebtclock.org, March 30th 2015. There were 86.365 million family groups in 2014, according to Table FG10, Families and Living Arrangements, from the US Census Bureau.

[57] Figure from Stockholm International Peace Research Institute.

CHAPTER 6
ENERGY QUESTIONS BUT FEW ANSWERS

OIL IN THE WATERS

Sun, moon, wind and water, and the Earth itself, are our energy futures, but the renewables lobby does not yet set the energy agenda. Oil, gas and coal remain indispensable to modern ways of life. The transport question looms. We are a long way from bulk freight transport powered by renewable electricity. For world trade to flourish, freight transport by sea is irreplaceable – and the solar powered merchant ship has yet to be invented. Almost all large surface ships have diesel engines.

Alternative, nuclear-powered cargo ships have been tried. The NS Savannah, funded by the US Government, was a cargo-passenger ship in service for ten years between 1962 and 1972. A German ship, the Otto Hahn, served for longer, 1960 to 1979, but then diesel engines replaced the nuclear reactor, and the ship continued under diesel power until it was scrapped in 2009. Japan also had a nuclear-powered ship, the Mutsu, in use from 1972 to 1992, but it was not deployed on cargo routes. Otherwise, nuclear-powered ships are either submarines or icebreakers.

Engineers are searching for alternatives to diesel. The Royal Academy of Engineering's report, *Future Ship Powering Options: Exploring alternative methods of ship propulsion*, published in July 2013, considers liquid petroleum gas (LPG), gas turbines, biofuels, solid oxide and molten carbonate fuel cells, hydrogen fuel cells, compressed air, liquid nitrogen, nuclear power, battery power, and hybrid systems. No perfect solutions exist. Batteries could be used in small ships on short runs, if there is power for recharging stations.

Hydrogen power would demand a global infrastructure, and for any growth in the number of nuclear-powered ships an efficient global emergency response system would be essential. Liquid nitrogen raises questions of tank design and size, as well as of an infrastructure network. Research has to go on, because diesel fuel from fossil oil will not be available indefinitely, and there is insufficient agricultural land for biodiesel to replace more than small fraction of conventional diesel. The runes are pointing to more sparing use of energy to power ships, and thus to less world trade.

Nuclear Obligations

In 2005 the then-Prime Minister Tony Blair refused to rule out a new generation of nuclear power stations to replace the UK's ageing stations, which were and are nearing the end of their life. At that point, nearly a quarter of electricity came from nuclear plants, around a third from coal-burning power stations, and well over a third from power plants burning natural gas. The balance of UK-generated power, about 7%, was from all other energy forms including oil. Four years later in 2009 the nuclear plants comprised 19 operating reactors generating 18% of the UK's electricity consumption of 371 billion kWh. In 2014 the number of working reactors was down to 16. All but one of these reactors were due to be closed down by 2023, when one new nuclear plant, at Hinkley Point C, might be operating.[1] The consortium behind Hinkley Point C, led by EDF Energy of France, includes China National Nuclear Corporation and China General Nuclear Power Corporation.

The Sustainable Development Commission[2] considered the pros and cons of a new generation of nuclear power stations and in 2006 issued a position paper, *The Role of Nuclear Power in a Low Carbon Economy*, which came down against the nuclear option.

"The conclusion from the analysis was that the UK could meet our CO_2 reduction targets and energy needs without nuclear power, using a combination of demand reduction, renewables, and more efficient use of fossil fuels combined with carbon capture and storage technologies."[3]

The commission had grave doubts about the safety of decommissioning nuclear power stations and storing waste, and about the ethics of imposing responsibilities for nuclear waste management on future generations. Members reckoned that a nuclear power programme "could divert public funding away from more sustainable technologies that will be needed regardless, hampering other long-term efforts to move to a low carbon economy with diverse energy sources". The paper also made the point that "[i]f the UK cannot meet its climate change commitments without nuclear power, then under the terms of the Framework Convention on Climate Change, we cannot deny others the same technology". Instead, said the commission, it would be preferable to use decentralised, small-scale energy generating technologies.

The "majority view" of the 16-strong commission, chaired by Jonathon Porritt and composed mainly of environmental and sustainability professionals, was that "there is no justification for bringing forward plans for a new nuclear power programme, at this time, and that any such proposal would be incompatible with the Government's own Sustainable Development Strategy". Careful not to box the government right into a corner, a majority of commission members also recommended that government should "continue to assess the potential contribution of new nuclear technologies for the future, as well as pursuing answers to our nuclear waste problems as actively as possible". This diluted the message somewhat, but even so the Labour government of the time did its best to forget about the report and its main recommendations.

The Sustainable Development Commission, set up in 2000 by the Blair government of 1997-2001, and given a higher profile and more resources in 2006, was axed by the Conservative-Liberal Democrat Coalition government in 2010 and closed on March 31st 2011.

The Blair government's own energy review,[4] published in July 2006, advocated a new generation of nuclear power stations for the

UK. Individuals would lose the right to object to a new nuclear plant on principle, and would be able to comment only on the suitability or otherwise of the proposed site. The same loss of rights to object would also apply to proposals for wind farms. The Infrastructure Planning Commission was to have been responsible for deciding on major planning projects like power stations, but in 2010 the incoming Coalition government opted to abolish it and to retain ministers' power to decide on planning issues of national importance.

The official British government line on paying for nuclear power plants remains a determination that the private sector must pay to build, operate and decommission them, but this is not quite the reality. The Nuclear Decommissioning Authority is funding the clean-up and storage of the UK's old reactors, and in 2014-15 has a budget of £3.228 billion, £2.236 billion of which comes from government.[5] In the USA typical decommissioning costs per reactor, after a productive life of about 30 years, exceed £200 million. These sums highlight the huge problem with nuclear power generation, the necessity of managing the residue in perpetuity, no matter what it costs.

By 2014 governments were in a quandary that had more to do with fossil-fuel depletion than with climate change: they needed, somehow, to keep the lights on. Their thoughts turned to ways of increasing private investment in nuclear power, and to the use of a high carbon price to discourage investment in high-emission energy and to encourage investment in renewables and nuclear power. The Treasury and Her Majesty's Revenue & Customs (HMRC) had outlined government thinking in their December 2010 consultation document, *Carbon price floor: support and certainty for low-carbon investment*, which proposed setting 'carbon price support rates' for levies on all fossil fuels, at a sufficiently high level to persuade the fuel and power industries and energy users to switch to renewables and nuclear. The document suggested that this could be done without substantial price rises. In fact, it proposed that the average annual household electricity bill would have risen by between £3 and £23 a year by 2020 but in 2030 would be between £20 and £48 lower than in 2009, at constant prices, because a plentiful supply of 'clean' electricity would push prices down. This forecast has echoes of the early, unfulfilled claims made for nuclear power, that it would be too cheap to meter. The calculations made by the Treasury and by HMRC omitted the permanent maintenance and storage obligations resulting from nuclear power, and the potentially lethal consequences of accidents and of aggressive uses of uranium to threaten, maim and kill.

DEPLETING URANIUM

The nuclear fission technology on which nuclear power generation currently depends is based around the heavy, unstable nucleus of uranium. When energy is added to this nucleus, it becomes more unstable and splits into two smaller nuclei as a result of electrostatic repulsion created by the large number of positively charged protons contained in a heavy nucleus. The process starts a fission chain reaction, which is too dangerous to initiate unless special neutron-absorbing fuel rods are used in reactors.

The feedstock for commercial nuclear power generation is isotope $uranium_{235}$,[6] which accounts for only about 0.7% of all available uranium. While uranium is a plentiful element, it is generally found in such low concentrations that extraction would be unworkable or uneconomic. The largest extractable reserves are in Australia and Kazakhstan, which in 2011 had approximately 1.661 million and 629,000 tonnes respectively of the world total of 5.327 million tonnes that are economically extractable at a price of about US$130 per kilogram.[7] Annual world usage of about 62,000 tonnes in 2011 – a fall of 9 per cent in five years -- suggests that at existing consumption rates, there is enough uranium for about 86 years. The World Nuclear Association, the source of these figures, is confident that new finds and new technologies will ensure a continuous supply indefinitely into the future. There will probably be sufficient uranium to power reactors for a century or more, but at the cost of dangerous radioactivity in the future.[8]

Loss of public confidence in nuclear power, substantial since the Fukushima disaster of March 2011, moderated demand for uranium, and in June 2014 the price of uranium oxide was $61.7 a kilo, less than half the oft-quoted threshold of $130 a kilo at which extraction would be economic. The price recovered slightly in the second half of 2014 and in March 2015 was $87 a kilo – still below the threshold for profitable extraction.

Public sentiment suggests that oil prices would have to rise to far beyond easy affordability before nuclear power could become a popular option. Should this happen, uranium extraction would accelerate, despite the damage which uranium mining causes to the environment, including the release of the gas radon$_{222}$, and leakage of radioactivity and toxic metals into water supplies.

URANIUM ENRICHMENT: MULTIPLE BUT ENERGY INTENSIVE OPTIONS

The mined uranium has to be enriched before it is useful as reactor fuel. Enrichment of raw uranium, called 'yellowcake', is carried out at plants in 15 countries including the USA, Russia, Japan, France and the UK. This means, of course, that the yellowcake has to be transported huge distances to be processed, and the enriched fuel has to be shipped onwards to the reactor sites.

Uranium can be enriched by any of several techniques, to different concentrations according to the demands of specific reactor types. All large-scale processing has successive identical stages, or cascades, progressively increasing the concentration of uranium$_{235}$. At each stage, the tailings are returned to the previous stage for further processing. Enrichment techniques include thermal diffusion, gaseous diffusion, gas centrifuges and Zippe centrifuges. Thermal diffusion requires heat to diffuse lighter uranium$_{235}$ molecules towards a hot surface, while heavier uranium$_{238}$ molecules diffuse towards a cold surface. In gaseous diffusion the radioactive gas, uranium hexafluoride, is forced through semipermeable membranes. This achieves a slight separation between the uranium$_{235}$ and uranium$_{238}$ molecules, and is regarded as an 'old technology' method.

The gas centrifuge technique uses a large number of rotating cylinders in series and parallel formations. The heavier uranium$_{238}$ molecules travel to the outside of the cylinders, and the lighter uranium$_{235}$ molecules cluster in the centre. Centrifuges use less energy than gas diffusion. A variant called the Zippe centrifuge requires heat at the bottom of rotating cylinders, creating currents that move the lighter uranium$_{235}$ molecules up the cylinder to be collected by scoops, while the heavier uranium is collected at the bottom, to move on to the next cylinder in the series. Pakistan has used Zippe technology in its nuclear weapons programme. Iran and North Korea also use the technique.

Aerodynamic enrichment processes achieve diffusion driven by pressure gradients – like a centrifuge, but not rotating. Solid uranium hexafluoride is diluted with hydrogen or helium as a carrier gas, to improve the efficiency of the technique, but aerodynamic processes tend to consume a lot of energy, and the removal of waste heat is a problem. The Uranium Enrichment Corporation of South Africa and Industrias Nucleares do Brasil use aerodynamic processes, albeit different forms.

Yet another uranium enrichment method is electromagnetic isotope separation, by which the metallic uranium is vaporised and then ionised to positively charged ions, accelerated, and deflected by magnetic fields to collection nodes. This method requires mass spectrometers called calutrons. A calutron was used to make the nuclear bomb dropped on Hiroshima.

Laser processes have generated excitement in the nuclear industry. Two examples are AVLIS, Atomic Vapor Laser Isotope Separation, which ionises uranium$_{235}$ atoms and no others, and MLIS, Molecular Laser Isotope Separation. MLIS requires an infrared laser to be directed at uranium hexafluoride gas, targeting molecules that contain a uranium$_{235}$ atom. Another laser isolates a fluorine atom, leaving uranium pentafluoride which precipitates out of the gas.

107

Chemical techniques include CHEMEX, developed in France and reliant on the different propensities of uranium$_{235}$ and uranium$_{238}$ to change valency in oxidation and reduction. In Japan, the Asahi Chemical Company developed an ion-exchange process to enrich uranium, using similar chemistry but achieving separation on a proprietary resin ion-exchange column.

Plasma separation, based on plasma physics and using superconducting magnets, is yet another technique for uranium enrichment.[9]

The intense competition to develop more efficient enrichment processes has in the past been due to nations' desires to make nuclear weapons as much as to concerns about a collapse in energy supply. The residue of the enrichment process, mainly uranium$_{238}$ – called depleted uranium – often finds its way into military hands, for use as (exceptionally toxic) ammunition, regardless of whether the original process was for 'peaceful' or military purposes. Even 'peaceful' nuclear power is an aggressive technology because of the huge toxicity burden it imposes on future generations.

After enriched uranium fuel has been used up, it is dissolved in nitric acid to extract the plutonium created during the burning process. This reprocessing is a dangerous undertaking. The great majority of commercial reprocessing is carried out in France, by state-controlled Areva, formerly Cogema, at Cap de la Hague on the Cotentin peninsula (near the Channel Islands). Most of the rest is reprocessed at Sellafield, in Cumbria, England.

Savannah River, South Carolina, in the USA, is the site for a plant that might process mixed oxides of plutonium and uranium (MOX) into reactor fuel. The plutonium would come from the US military. Construction began late in 2005, but in May 2006 the House of Representatives voted against funding the venture. In August the following year, construction resumed. Work was due to finish in 2014, and operations to begin in 2016 and continue until 2035-2038. By 2013 costs exceeded $7.7 billion, and the federal government wanted to halt the project – but the state of South Carolina, anxious about job losses, threatened a lawsuit and construction carried on.

The estimated cost of building the plant and operating it for 20 years had by this time exceeded $30 billion.[10] The process would result in only a small reduction in the amount of residual plutonium, and using the mixed oxides to fuel nuclear reactors could reduce the stability of reactor cores, thus increasing the costs of reactor maintenance.

The processes of uranium mining and milling, its enrichment and conversion into fuel rods, and reprocessing, are energy intensive. The release of carbon dioxide into the atmosphere is another harmful by-product of the nuclear energy chain. Diesel-drinking trucks for uranium mining, power for crushing plants and pumping slurry, the use of energy-intensive products in uranium processing, like sulphuric acid, lime, amines, kerosene, ammonia, and the roasting of yellowcake in furnaces at 800 degrees C, all contribute to further global warming.[11] The treatment of radioactive waste, and transport to a dumping ground, also consume energy and emit greenhouse gases. The nuclear power industry requires a great deal of transport, which is still dependent on fossil fuels.

The technology of nuclear fission has advanced substantially since the early days, but it is not 'safe' and its dangers are long lasting. The common isotope plutonium$_{239}$ has a half-life of 24,360 years, for example. We cannot be sure that future generations will have the technology, or the resources, to monitor and contain nuclear waste.

Power distribution is another problematic factor that is too often taken for granted. Nuclear power stations are so expensive to construct that they can never be spread across the globe in local, environment-friendly networks. Nuclear plants have to 'plug in' to long-distance power transportation lines. Unless there is an assiduously maintained power grid, electricity generated from nuclear reaction has nowhere to go. The dependence of nuclear power on highly complex infrastructure systems is a major drawback that is not widely debated in public media. Nuclear power is an enslaving technology. Reactors have to be monitored constantly, and warning signals acted on immediately and correctly.

To cope with these constraints, workers need to be expert, and management to be watertight.

FAST BREEDER REACTORS: SHORT LIVES

The history of nuclear technology does not bode well for its future. Fast breeder reactors[12] (FBRs) use mixed oxide fuel of up to 20% plutonium dioxide and at least 80% uranium dioxide, which comes from reprocessed civil plutonium or dismantled nuclear weapons. Dounreay in northern Scotland had two fast breeder reactors: a test reactor, Dounreay Fast, which operated from 1959 to 1977, and Dounreay Prototype Fast, in use from 1975 to 1994. Thus each reactor was producing electricity for only a few years, considerably fewer years than the 'expected' life of a nuclear reactor, which is 30 to 60 years, depending on the particular technology and the optimism of the commissioning body. There were problems with the liquid sodium cooling system at Dounreay, which hastened closure. Yet the dismantling of Dounreay will take until about 2095 – over 100 years, compared with just 35 years of electricity from the two reactors. Environmental problems include nuclear fuel particles found on the sea bed, radiated and chemically contaminated land, 900 tonnes of radioactive sodium in a total of 1,500 tonnes of sodium, groundwater contamination, and nuclear waste in a shaft that within 300 years is likely to be threatened by coastal erosion.

The USA's first commercial fast breeder reactor, the Enrico Fermi at Lagoona Beach, Michigan, closed when the process was compromised by loose zirconium. The Superphénix FBR plant on the Rhône, in France near the Swiss border, using liquid sodium for cooling and heat transfer, ran just from 1984 to 1997, when it closed as a result of high costs and risky incidents. In December 1995, the Monju FBR reactor in Japan was shut down after a sodium leak. Short lives indeed.

PRESSURISED WATER REACTORS: WORLD MAJORITY INCLUDING CHERNOBYL

The name 'pressurised water reactor' (PWR) conveys an impression of simplicity, in that steam is transferred by heat exchanger to a secondary coolant, which reduces it to a temperature at which it is safe to generate electricity or propel a nuclear-powered boat. The World Nuclear Association reported that in 2012, 271 PWRs were in use, worldwide, for power generation, accounting for 62% of all reactors. In addition several hundred nuclear-powered vessels – typically large submarines – patrolled the world's oceans. But PWRs need uranium as fuel, and radioactive decay continues to generate large amounts of heat after the fission reaction has stopped, with the risk of reactor meltdown. The European Pressurised Reactor (EPR), new in the 21st century and of French-German design, has more safety features but still a need for costly care far into the future. The EPR, developed by Areva, EDF and Siemens, is making very slow headway. Four were under construction in 2014, in Finland, France, and two in China. The European ones are at least two years behind schedule. The two in China, at Taishan, Guangdong, were predicted to operate from 2014 and 2015 respectively, but neither had come on stream by the end of March 2015.

At Three Mile Island in Pennsylvania a pressurised water reactor[13] (PWR) suffered a partial meltdown of the core on March 28th 1979, and stirred anti-nuclear protest. In September that year 200,000 people staged an anti-nuclear march in New York, and there were other demonstrations of public hostility. It's impossible to say how influential these protests were. The civil nuclear programme in the USA has lagged, but the main reason for that is probably the huge current costs and unquantifiable future costs of nuclear power infrastructures. The layers of US government are tightening the screw on protest, even criminalising it, as in the case

111

of the nun, Sister Megan Rice, who in February 2014 was sentenced to 35 months in prison for an anti-nuclear peace protest.[14]

The most notorious nuclear accident up to 2011 was Chernobyl, on April 26th 1986. Chernobyl, then in the USSR, now in the territory of Ukraine, near the border with Belarus, was a plant using RBMK-1000 light water graphite reactors, a design built only in the USSR. Steam in reactor no.4 exploded, causing a fire that triggered more explosions, resulting in meltdown. In 2014 a 19-mile exclusion zone remained around Chernobyl, a zone which has become an unusual tourist attraction.[15]

ADVANCED GAS COOLED REACTORS: LIFE EXTENDED BEYOND ORIGINAL SAFETY THRESHOLD

Advanced gas cooled (AGR) reactors are yet another type of fission plant, achieving higher thermal efficiency than PWRs but hungrier for fuel. The UK had 14 advanced gas cooled reactors in 2010, on seven sites, developed from the earlier Magnox (Magnesium Non-Oxidising) reactor.[16] The number was the same in 2014. They provide between one sixth and one seventh of the UK's electricity supply and are thus critical to the stability of the nation. Early in 2014 EDF, operator of the power stations, made a £70-million-a-year agreement with infrastructure firm Doosan Babcock to extend their planned lives beyond the original closure dates, which were between 2014 and 2023. Life extensions, typically sought in two five-year tranches, are not without risk. For example, at Dungeness B on the south coast of England, the maximum weight loss of the graphite bricks at the core of the reactor was 6.2%. Above that, there is a danger that in case of need to shut down the reactor, the control rods could not be inserted, making shut-down impossible. EDF applied to raise the safety threshold to 8% weight loss, necessary if power generation is to continue. It is impossible to replace the bricks, which are damaged in use by intense radiation bombardment and by the effects of the carbon dioxide coolant. No one really knows the 'safe' limit for the bricks' weight loss. Professor

William Nuttall, professor of energy at the Open University and fellow of Hughes Hall, University of Cambridge, says carefully, "the UK effort to extend the life of AGR reactors involves the exploration of much new territory."[17]

MORE DOUBTS AND RISKS

Huge questions remain about the sources of Great Britain's electricity after 2035, when the most recent of the island's nuclear power stations, the pressurised water reactor Sizewell B, is scheduled to close after 40 years of operation.

Replacing just one nuclear power station could cost £4.8 billion, excluding waste management and decommissioning costs, according to an energy company chief back in 2008.[18] The sum today could well exceed £6 billion.

Renewed doubts about the safety of nuclear power spread after the crippling of the Fukushima Daiichi nuclear plant in Japan, during the earthquake and tsunami of March 11th 2011. The alarmed public heard the news of three wrecked cores; hundreds of tons of 'liberated' uranium, plutonium, caesium and strontium; and 300 to 400 tonnes of contaminated radioactive groundwater reaching the Pacific Ocean daily.[19] There was no public appetite in Japan for a resumption of nuclear power, but in 2014 the government, lacking other secure energy supplies, began the process of re-opening the country's nuclear plants, which had been shut down after the Fukushima accident. After the disaster, Japan's imports of liquefied natural gas soared 23%, and imports of oil rose 16%, leading to steep energy price hikes, up to 50% more for businesses.

Around Fukushima, 140,000 people remained evicted from the 12-mile exclusion zone surrounding the plant. The interior of the complex itself was still off-limits in 2014. No one had ventured inside: it was far too dangerous.

Government breakdowns and warfare are threats to future nuclear safety, risks largely absent from mass media which prioritise 'infotainment' such as tittle-tattle about 'celebrities'. The risks of a nuclear accident at the same time as other failures – of the power grid, of transport networks, of the financial system – are glossed over. The astronomer Sir Martin Rees, former president of the Royal Society and Master of Trinity College, Cambridge, raises awareness of risk in articles such as 'We are in denial about catastrophic risk',[20] in which he argues that we should adopt a much more cautious approach to the risks of applying new technologies.

NUCLEAR FUSION'S €17.5 BILLION TRIAL...AND COUNTING

Uranium fuel for fission processes, potentially so dangerous, generates electricity for about five years and then has to be replaced. Thorium could potentially replace uranium as a fuel for nuclear fission. It is more abundant, and wastes are fewer and less troublesome. Thorium is, though, a long way from commercialisation as nuclear fuel.

The technology of nuclear fusion would avoid the hazards of uranium fuel, although fusion is still experimental. In nuclear fusion, two light nuclei combine to form a single heavier nucleus. The most promising experimentation has been with the hydrogen isotopes deuterium and tritium, which fuse to form helium, in the process releasing vast quantities of energy.

Commercial fusion will depend on the construction of reactors at enormous cost, capable of operating at temperatures exceeding 100 million degrees Centigrade. It is alarming to imagine such heat, let alone to consider how to eliminate risk from fusion reactions.

Yet governments are determined to try and develop nuclear fusion. Their growing nervousness about future energy shortages – a concern that they still try to conceal from the public – is clear from the decision, in June 2005, of the European Union, the USA, Russia, China, Japan and South Korea, to invest in the International Thermonuclear Experimental Reactor (ITER), a tokamak reactor under construction but by 2014 two years behind schedule, in France at Cadarache, less than 40 miles from Marseilles. India joined the original investors in this hugely expensive project, which in mid-

2010 had a price tag of €16 billion and in 2014 €17.5 billion, €7.9 billion of which has to be found by the European Union.

The tokamak, which uses a magnetic field to confine a plasma in a torus (giving a shape similar to a doughnut), and which is probably the front runner in emerging fusion technologies, was invented in the Soviet Union in the 1950s by Igor Tamm and by Andre Sakharov, who later became one of Soviet Russia's most active human rights dissidents, and died of a heart attack in 1989, aged 68. The tokamak under construction in France is the largest ever built and will weigh 23,000 tons. Inside, the temperature should reach 150 million degrees Centigrade, ten times greater than at the core of the sun.

The big arguments in favour of fusion using deuterium and tritium are economy and cleanliness. One gram of deuterium would, according to experts' calculations, yield the same amount of energy as more than three tonnes of coal. A pick-up truck full of deuterium could release energy equivalent to 10 million barrels of oil.[21] Both deuterium and tritium can be isolated from seawater, and there would be no supply shortages. The problem is that the process is a long way from practical reality, and even if the trial ITER reactor can be replicated, the technology itself would require continuous expert management, and all forces of nature would have to be neutralised.

Nuclear power, whether by fission or fusion, would not fit into the localised agrarian economies which I believe we will need in future if we are once again to feed ourselves sustainably. Nuclear power is a hyper-industrial technology that demands an energy-intensive infrastructure built and maintained to exact technical specifications, an infrastructure that our descendants would need to manage safely for millennia. We cannot know whether they will have the resources – the skills, knowledge, materials and money -- to accomplish the task. Do we really want the world littered with decommissioned nuclear plants, dangerous monuments demanding permanent care in return for a few short years of electricity?

COAL AND THE CARBON STORAGE CONUNDRUM

Coal is still very big business. Worldwide, around 40% of electricity is generated from coal, and nearly 70% of world steel production depends on coal.[22] In agriculture, coal is of direct benefit principally as fuel to generate electricity.

The UK has a fair amount of coal, proven reserves of about 400 million tonnes,[23] but as consumption is around 60 million tonnes, if imports dried up the current reserves would not last seven years. In any case, coal is a dirty fuel, and even with 'clean' technology generates electricity at no more than 45% efficiency.

The main argument heard against burning coal is its contribution to global warming. Technologies to reduce emissions from coal-fired industrial sites include coal washing to reduce ash and sulphur dioxide; use of electrostatic precipitators and fabric filters, again to reduce ash; desulphurisation to cut sulphur dioxide emissions by over 95% in the most successful cases; and special burners to reduce nitrogen oxide emissions by up to 40%.[24]

Then there is carbon dioxide capture and storage. The European Commission was in 2012 casting around for carbon capture and storage trial projects to support, but there were none, save for the 'White Rose' project from the UK. The EU granted this £250 million. The scheme involves a new coal-fired power station next to Drax at Selby, North Yorkshire, the capture of two million tonnes of carbon dioxide a year, 90% of the total, and its deposition below the North Sea. Meanwhile the original Drax station is converting from coal- to biomass-fired.[25]

Commercial electricity generators do not seem enthusiastic about carbon storage. E.ON, the German power company which had planned a new coal-fired power station with carbon capture and storage at Kingsnorth in Kent, abandoned the project in October 2010, despite the chance of obtaining up to £1 billion from the Treasury as part of government plans to clean up electricity generation.[26] The original Kingsnorth power station then closed down, in 2013.

'Clean coal' accompanied by carbon dioxide burial could serve as an interim technology while renewables are developed, but the danger would be that power generators, and nations, cling to it for too long, treating it as a replacement for oil- and gas-fired power generation instead of as a temporary stop-gap.

The United Nations' Intergovernmental Panel on Climate Change reported [27] that storing carbon dioxide could make a 30% contribution to the efforts needed to limit emissions of the gas into the atmosphere. The gas would be returned – by pipeline injection -- into the earth. A major drawback is the energy costs of capture: a power plant with carbon dioxide capture would consume between 10% and 40% more energy than one without capture. In the mid-2000s the mooted costs per tonne of carbon capture and storage were between $150 and $220. In 2014 the estimated range was $60 to $90 per tonne – less, but still substantial.[28]

The technology is still in an early phase, but seen as a possible saviour by governments and corporations. Yet carbon dioxide deep in the Earth's crust may be out of sight and out of mind, but the crust has a habit of moving, sinking, crushing and splitting. It is restless, just like the atmosphere. Carbon dioxide would probably remain as a supercritical gas for thousands of years, during which time its earthly tomb could open up. Gas injection would, of course, also require a highly complex and costly logistics network to carry the carbon dioxide to its subterranean vault.

ABIOGENIC OIL AND GAS: CLUTCHING A STRAW?

In the 1980s Thomas Gold,[29] astronomy professor at Cornell University in the USA, proposed that hydrocarbons form in a zone between about 60 miles and 180 miles below the earth's surface, in the mantle, and then move upwards, acquiring complex organic attributes on the way, and refilling depleted oil and gas fields. Professor Gold set out his theory in 'The deep, hot biosphere', a paper in the Proceedings of the National Academy of Sciences in 1992, and in his book *The Deep Hot Biosphere* in 1999.[30] His hypothesis, building on research by scientists in the Russian and

117

Ukrainian soviet republics in the 1950s, excites interest from those who are worried about the declining availability of fossil fuels.

Enthusiasts for the prospect of this oil, called inorganic, abiotic or abiogenic,[31] include Stanley Keith, of geological consulting company MagmaChem. Stanley Keith is fascinated by the chemistry around ocean fissures such as 'Lost City', some ten miles from the crest of the Mid Atlantic Ridge, where methane and bacteria abound at the mineral-encrusted vents. The bacteria subsist on methane that is produced by 'serpentization', reactions of the ocean water with rock rich in magnesium or silicon, down in the fissures. Stanley Keith suggests that plate tectonics lead to the formation of inorganic oil, when oceanic crust, containing what he calls 'hydrothermal brine' has been forced below continental land masses. In this hypothesis, the brine reacts with rocks in the Earth's mantle to form hydrogen and methane, which change into more complex hydrocarbons as they cool.

Professor Barbara Sherwood Lollar of the University of Toronto, while agreeing that abiogenic hydrocarbons exist, offers a different hypothesis. She reckons that the Earth's mantle is not necessarily involved in the process of methane production which, according to her research, results from water and rock interactions above the mantle, in the crust.

The geological profession is divided, not so much over the formation of abiogenic oil, but about its quantities and recoverability. Stanley Keith is more optimistic than Barbara Sherwood Lollar about the chances of locating large, extractable deposits, but even if inorganic hydrocarbons should emerge as a plentiful resource they would not rescue energy-intensive civilisation. Burning inorganic hydrocarbons would, just like burning organic hydrocarbons, release carbon dioxide into the atmosphere, adding to global warming and climatic instability. Even abiogenic methane hydrate, which contains less carbon than abiogenic oil, comes with considerable attendant problems. The escape of large quantities of methane gas into the atmosphere would be catastrophic because methane is twenty times more powerful than carbon dioxide as a cause of global warming,[32] and has global warming potential 86 times greater over 20 years, 34 times over 100 years.[33] Escaped methane would make flying less safe because the gas could cause planes to explode. Methane also reduces the density of water so that ships − and oil rigs -- could sink. The capacity of land and water to support life as we know it would decline. Do we want another Venus, where the surface temperature is over 870 degrees Fahrenheit, hot enough to melt lead?

HYDROGEN HOPES

The tiny Norwegian island of Utsira, a speck just six kilometres square in the North Sea and home to about 235 people, has a hydrogen economy − or rather a wind economy supported by hydrogen. When there is surplus wind energy, the excess is used to generate hydrogen by electrolysis.[34] A hydrogen engine and a fuel cell convert the hydrogen back to electricity when there is no wind. But Utsira is a windy place, and the power generated is for local use. The hydrogen does not have to travel far. A hydrogen-and-wind economy is suited to islands and other self-contained windy locations, and is developing in the Faroe Islands, the Hebrides and the Shetlands. The Shetland island of Unst is home to Pure Energy, a pioneer research and development centre for renewable hydrogen technologies.

Hydrogen is clean in use but also diffuse, leaky and inefficient. Fossil fuels − coal, oil, natural gas -- are the feedstock for the great majority of hydrogen manufacture. Hydrogen is bulky to store[35] -- three times bulkier than natural gas for the same amount of energy delivered -- and also bulky to transport. Hydrogen accelerates the cracking (and thus replacement) of steel transport pipes. Leaking hydrogen could form free radicals[36] under the influence of ultra violet radiation in the stratosphere. These free radicals could be catalysts for further depletion of ozone, which protects life on Earth from harmful ultra-violet radiation. About half of manufactured hydrogen is destined for ammonia, a step in the production of fertiliser. The fertiliser boosts crop yields artificially, enabling farmers to deplete soil fertility without immediately experiencing lower yields. Much of the rest of the manufactured hydrogen is used for hydrocracking,[37] converting heavy petroleum into lighter products suitable as fuels, thus accelerating global warming by adding to carbon dioxide emissions.

It seemed for a while that the USA's Department of Energy was going to invest more than nominally in hydrogen fuel cell technology, but the allocated funding was slashed by about 60% in 2011, to $70 million. Work continues but at a slower pace than between 2000 and 2010. Meanwhile, South Korean and Japanese vehicle manufacturers intensified their research. South Korea's Hyundai launched the ix35 hydrogen car in 2013, and intended to produce 1,000 by 2015, then ramping up to 10,000. Both Honda and Toyota of Japan intend to have hydrogen fuel cell vehicles in production in 2015.[38]

TIDES AND WAVES

A turbine placed in a fast tidal current in seawater, which is 900 times denser than air,[39] can generate significant amounts of power. Tidal power, courtesy of the moon, has much potential for coastal regions, but is less relevant for areas far inland, because of power losses in transmission. Tides are still barely exploited as a source of power, although the world's first tidal power station was built at La Rance, Brittany, France, back in the early 1960s. There is a pioneer in-stream tidal current generator at Race Rocks, Vancouver Island in Canada, and in the UK a small 1.2MW tidal power plant at Strangford Lough in Northern Ireland, tiny compared with the 240MW at La Rance.

Several mega-schemes are under consideration worldwide, notably in South Korea, where the first stage of the Jindo Uldolmok plant was constructed between 2009 and 2011, and should ultimately have an installed capacity of 90MW. Seven more big tidal power plants are an important part of South Korea's plans to ramp up electricity generation from renewables. The country is a peninsula and has only one land border, with North Korea.

The UK's newly elected Coalition government axed, in October 2010, plans for tidal power generation in the Severn estuary, which had been projected to provide up to 5% of the nation's electricity, on the grounds that the likely cost of £30 billion would be too great, and that they believed wind and nuclear power would be cheaper.

Wave power uses the force in sea waves rather than the rise and fall of water levels in tides. The UK's first wave-power station was constructed on the island of Islay, one of the Inner Hebrides off the west coast of Scotland, and is a 500kW scheme operated by Wavegen, part of Voith Hydro within the German company Voith AG.

Wavegen, which also has a wave-power station on the Faroe Islands, reckons that wave power from the seas around the UK could eventually generate enough electricity to meet domestic needs.[40] Use of the technology is growing, and moving to larger islands, but not without setbacks. Voith had the contract to build the Siadar Wave Energy Project on the island of Lewis in the Outer Hebrides. This plant, to generate up to 4MW, would have been operated by npower renewables, a subsidiary of the German group RWE Innogy within RWE Group. Despite its promise, the project was axed in 2013 due to funding uncertainties.

The potential for water power overall is widely ignored. In centuries past, power from streams turned water wheels, but most were left to rot early in the age of electricity. Small-scale water power has great local possibilities again, although complicated by bureaucratic rules and restrictions. In the UK, for example, abstraction licences are mandatory, even when the water is returned undamaged into the water course from whence it came.

WIND WOBBLES

Wind power varies so much that in most areas it cannot be the sole power source. Even in the United Kingdom, in the path of strong air flows streaming over the Atlantic from the west and the windiest place in Europe, wind alone could not provide a steady stream of electricity, hour after hour. If wind farms covered 4% of the UK's land area, 9,715 square kilometres,[41] they could in theory provide sufficient electricity, but not evenly enough -- an excess during gales, insufficient during calm periods. Winds become stronger with distance from the ground, so wind farm operators go for the highest possible mast height, thus the turbines are visible for many miles around. Planning applications for wind farms often spark strong opposition from people living nearby, worried about noise from whirring turbines and damage to property values. Peering into the future, the Gulf Stream and the westerly winds associated with it could decline or even disappear as a result of climate change. Large wind farms might then be sited in completely the wrong places.

Applications for wind farms create conflict in the countryside, conflicts that are hard to tackle and even harder to resolve, as the following three extracts from my blog 'West Wales News Review' attempt to show.

Wind Blows Uncertainty into the Carmarthenshire Countryside

"Eight groups opposed to wind farms in Carmarthenshire sent representatives to Llansawel Village Hall yesterday (April 24th 2014) to talk about setting up a united steering group to campaign for compensation to be paid to owners of properties devalued by nearby wind turbines. It was a very polite meeting, but after two hours of discussion there was still no steering group, a decision deferred to a future meeting.

Wind has blown uncertainty into the Carmarthenshire countryside, where wind turbines are multiplying with such speed that coherent analysis of their impacts is always out of date. There is no 'plan' as such — the generating companies search for landowners willing to work with them, and then apply for planning permissions. Residents never know if a wind farm may be coming to them. In theory, wind farms should be confined to 'TAN 8' areas, allocated for energy production by the Welsh Government in Technical Advice Note 8, Renewable Energy, dated 2005. But increasingly, planning applications are for turbines on sites well out of TAN 8 zones. Most of these applications can be determined in Wales, but for really big wind farms, producing at least 50MW of electricity, the yay or nay comes from London.

The anti-turbine action groups include many diligent people arguing points of view that conflict with government priorities. They are vulnerable to being called NIMBYs,[42] because people whose environments are unaffected by masts hundreds of feet high think 'they've got to go somewhere'. There is no getting away from our need for renewable energy, both to trim emissions of greenhouse gases and to maintain electricity supplies as the era of cheap fossil fuels draws to a close. This latter point was not considered by anyone at yesterday's meeting.

If local communities benefited directly from wind turbines, and if the generators were social enterprises rather than multinational corporations which distribute profits elsewhere in the UK, or outside the UK completely, often in tax havens, there would probably be more support for wind farms. If small wind farms supplied power to the communities in which they are located, they could in time be accepted as indispensable.

The issue of using power close to its source is important because new transmission lines are disruptive, costly, and they leak. Wind farms located in hilly rural areas tend to be distant from large population centres, and thus transmission power losses add further to the cost of the electricity produced.

The cultural divisions created by wind farms in rural Wales are real but under-reported. Landowners who receive payments for turbines on their land are often Welsh-speaking farmers. With possible rent per turbine of up to £40,000 or so a year, if a landowner hosts 15 large turbines that's about £600,000 a year, akin to winning the lottery over and over again. Objectors are often

– not always – retirees from England, whose long-dreamed rural idyll is rudely shattered. While their farmer neighbours scoop the financial jackpot, they receive nothing to compensate for the loss of their tranquil retirement. That does not foster good community relations. The opposite, in fact.

If local communities had real ownership of energy plans, we could soon be moving forward with less antagonism, less anger, than now. It's tough for the action groups trying to protect their local hill tops, groups like Mynydd Llansadwrn Action Group (MLAG); Residents Against Turbines (RATs) from Five Roads; Villages Against Supersize Turbines (VAST), in and around Llansawel and Rhydcymerau; Brechfa Forest Energy Action Group (BFEAG); Grwp Blaengwen at Gwyddgrug; Llandovery Anti Turbine Action Group (LATAG); Caio Against Wind Turbines (CAWT); and more. They are separate small groups facing large corporations and big government, and the odds are stacked against them. All the time that huge payments are offered to landowners, the communities they are part of will fragment, and the losers will press for financial compensation."

published April 25th 2014 as 'Local energy plans should help prevent wind wars', amended March 31st 2015

Can any big industrial development really be called 'green'? The next extract from 'West Wales News Review' considers the bias towards mega-projects which are imposed on communities.

IS WIND POWER REALLY ALL THAT GREEN?

"Wind woes continue to spread over north Carmarthenshire. Public meetings to tell local people about the scale of turbines intended for Nantyrast, Rhandirmwyn and Tyllwyd, Cwrt y Cadno, are packed but quiet, as the seated rows take in the implications of masts 480 feet high.

The latest venue, yesterday March 17th, was in the (closed) village primary school at Cilycwm, some three miles down the Tywi valley from Rhandirmwyn. About 70 people jammed into a former classroom to hear Sir David Lewis, former Lord Mayor of the City of London, outline the planning and environmental objections to a 36-turbine wind power 'station' above the upper Cothi and upper Tywi valleys.

While Sir David, who lives in Cwrt y Cadno, is strongly opposed to such an industrial-scale development, a second cousin with the same surname farms the land on which 26 of the 36 turbines would be constructed. Big money is at stake, perhaps £40,000 a year per turbine. This would almost certainly be split between the Crown Commissioners, who are the landowners, and three farmers who have said they may be willing to host the turbines and who have tenancies on the land.

The Cambrian Mountains Society, squarely against giant wind power installations, was represented at the meeting by their chair, Ann West, who stressed the community divisions which opened up when a few people were offered sums of lottery-win dimensions while most received no compensation at all for damage to their environment and way of life.

The story of the mooted wind turbines, on the quiet hills west of Llyn Brianne, would be one of money flowing out of the area, of 1,000 tonnes or more of concrete for each base, of new roads and of miles of pylons, in the case of Nantyrast and Tyllwyd all the way down to Swansea. There would be inescapable noise audible over some six miles, and the landscape would change from rural to industrial. The Welsh Government has not designated the area for wind turbines, but permission for wind-power generation on this scale would be given in London, not in Wales – unless energy policy becomes a devolved power in double-quick time.

As yet there is no planning application, and so nothing to object to, but the idea behind the public meetings is to tell people what to expect, and to advise on the actions that can be taken if and when an application is submitted. "Don't do anything yet," Sir David counselled.

We are in strange times, in need of energy, but government focuses on investment from mega businesses, and gives little encouragement to small-scale, sensitive community schemes. If there were more backing for local energy schemes – hydro and solar as well as limited wind – public attitudes should be much more favourable.

Community schemes are beginning to emerge. Egni, the South Wales Valleys Solar Photovoltaic Co-operative, is one. Egni (Welsh for 'energy') is a co-operative which aims to put photovoltaic panels on community buildings in South Wales, including Brynaman Public Hall and Cinema. This is energy for the community, not profits destined for elsewhere (notably tax havens), and seems an altogether more promising path to take."

published March 18th 2014 as 'Solar co-op is greener than big wind'

Large wind farms and tax havens have more than a nodding acquaintance, as residents in north Carmarthenshire heard in February 2014.

PUBLIC INVESTMENT, PRIVATE PROFITS – GOOD NEWS FOR TAX HAVENS

"Wind energy is generously subsidised by us, through the Renewables Obligation component of our electricity bills. This system is due to last only until March 31st 2017, when Contracts for Difference should replace Renewables Obligation Certificates. The user will still pay, but rather than a fixed levy, the amount on the bill will reflect the difference between the price when the contract was signed and the price at the time of use. If the price has gone up, the

user pays the difference. Should the price go down, the seller would refund the difference.

The Treasury intends to reduce contract prices. For onshore wind, the 2015-16 price would be £95 per MW hour, and in 2017-18, £90, which would be £50 per MW/hr less than for offshore wind, £20 less than for large-scale solar, and £15 less than for biomass.

Given the Treasury's intentions to cut support for renewable energy (except biomass), it's no surprise that generating companies are super-keen to get projects on stream before the end of March 2017, when the Renewables Obligation scheme is scheduled to end.

This dash for wind brings us to the upper Cothi valley in Carmarthenshire and to rumours of a large wind farm for the generating company Infinis Energy plc. It is known that some farmers in the upper reaches of the valley, where the bare Cambrian Mountains dominate the landscape west of Llyn Brianne, have been asked if they are interested in having turbines on the land they farm. The land itself is owned by the Crown Estates, which holds it on behalf of the Queen, and pays its revenue surplus to the Treasury.

Some 100 people from the upper Cothi area sat quietly in Pumsaint's Coronation Hall on Wednesday February 5th to hear Sir David Lewis outline the likelihood of a wind farm on the Cambrian hill tops.

Sir David, a corporate finance lawyer with the firm Norton Rose, formerly chair and senior partner, now consultant, and Lord Mayor of the City of London in 2007-08, lives at Cwrt y Cadno and so is very well placed to know about wind farm possibilities in the surrounding hills.

Infinis Energy is seeking sites for 36 turbines, Sir David told the meeting. The power cables from the wind farm would stretch from pylon to pylon down to Pumsaint and onwards to Llansawel, then to connect with the power transmission network from the wind farms in Brechfa Forest.

High-voltage cables could go underground, but research suggests that the cost could be in the range £10.2 million to £24.1 million per kilometre, according to data from the Institution of Engineering and

Technology which was included in a notice from the Campaign to Protect Rural England. Overhead high-voltage lines, according to the same notice, typically cost £2.2 million to £4.2 million per kilometre.

Electricity is best generated close to its consumers, to minimise transmission costs and problems, but the upper Cothi is remote and sparsely populated. With wind power, the transmission grid will be unused when there is no wind. The longer the transmission lines, the greater the 'wasted' costs of under-utilisation.

The Welsh Government identified, in Technical Advice Note 8, 'strategic areas' for wind farms. Brechfa is one of these, Strategic Area G, but the upper Cothi is not in an identified strategic area. However, as the decision whether or not to allow a wind farm here would be taken by the UK government, and not in Cardiff, the 'strategic area' designations might not carry much weight.

Infinis Energy plc, the company apparently seeking sites in the upper Cothi valley, is currently 68.56% owned by Monterey Capital II S.a.r.L, based in Luxembourg. Monterey Capital II is controlled by a chain of companies, in turn controlled by Mr Guy Hands, who lives in Guernsey. Until flotation on the London Stock Exchange in November 2013, Mr Hands' control of the company was even more emphatic.

Profit and loss figures mean little when a company is controlled by a private equity entity, but when members of the public can buy and sell shares, they should be fairly confident that the company is aiming to be profitable. Will Infinis Energy plc be consistently profitable? The business made a pre-tax loss of £7.60 million in the year to end-March 2013, and another pre-tax loss, £4.91 million, in the six months to end-September 2013.

Yet Infinis Energy plc's predecessor, Infinis Holdings, made a £44.3 million dividend payment to Monterey Capital II S.a.r.L at the end of the March-September reporting period. Infinis Holdings' share capital was then acquired in its entirety by Infinis Energy Ltd, which re-registered as Infinis Energy plc on October 28th 2013, prior to flotation.

If Infinis does apply to build a wind farm in the upper Cothi, and at present it is 'if' and not 'when', a sizeable chunk of any profits would, it appears from the ownership structure, be destined for tax havens — Luxembourg, via Monterey Capital II, and then quite possibly Guernsey."

published as 'Onshore wind blows profits offshore', February 6th 2014

Recycling Waste

Methane energy from livestock excrement is another electrical possibility, as a single cow can emit 600 litres of methane a day, enough to generate two kilowatts of electricity. Capturing the gas in an anaerobic digester, and using it as fuel for electricity generation, has a high capital cost, typically between £100,000 and £200,000 for an on-farm digester.[43] From an environmental perspective, it would be better to cut livestock farming drastically and grow more crops instead, to produce more food per hectare and cut down methane emissions. We would still need livestock for the mixed farming that needs to replace monocultures, but in smaller numbers, and so mini methane-to-electricity systems would be useful additions to the micro-generation portfolio. Methane from landfill gas is another option for electricity generation.[44]

Thermal depolymerization has potential for producing oil from complex organic wastes, and this technology has been used commercially in Carthage, Missouri. Renewable Environmental Solutions' plant took turkey waste from Smithfield Foods' Butterball Turkey plant in the locality, and manufactured it into oil. The process was complex and energy-intensive, involving the breakdown of long-chain polymers of hydrogen, oxygen and carbon into short-chain petroleum hydrocarbons. The plant produced about 400 barrels of oil a day, at a cost of about $80 a barrel and efficiency of around 85%. For thermal depolymerization to replace geological oil, coal and gas, virtually all organic wastes would have to be processed in this way, a possibility that is not feasible in the short or medium term. The Carthage plant was not typical, either, because it relied on 200 tons of turkey waste per day -- some 73,000 tons a year -- from the huge adjacent food factory.

The plant closed in April 2009 when Renewable Environmental Solutions' parent Changing World Technologies Inc filed for bankruptcy, but Ridgeline Energy Services of Canada acquired Changing World Technologies in 2013 and took over the plant.

GROUND HEAT IS ALREADY HERE

Ground source heat pumps are another heating possibility and have a lot in their favour. They require electricity to function but are more than four times as efficient as a boiler and should last 25 years, about twice as long as a well-maintained boiler. The systems require a fair amount of cash, typically between £9,000 and £17,000, according to the UK's Energy Saving Trust.[45] Their main benefit is not financial, but the substantially reduced carbon emissions from domestic heating, for example for a three-bedroomed home the reduction is about 4,985 kilograms of CO_2 a year compared with electric heating. The energy return on energy invested is typically a ratio of between 3 and 4 to one.

A ground source heat pump changes low-temperature energy in the ground to higher-temperature energy via a refrigeration process. The source heat is collected in a loop of plastic pipes that are laid below ground horizontally or, where land is limited, vertically in bore holes up to 200 metres deep. Heat pumps overall have been under-exploited in Britain except in fridges. They work by driving a fluid round a refrigeration circuit containing four elements: an evaporator, a compressor, a condenser, and an expansion valve. The fluid changes from liquid to gas as heat is absorbed from the heat source. Later in the cycle, the fluid condenses to liquid as heat is released where it is required. Heat pumps have an expected life of about 20 years and the ground collection system maybe 70 years, advises the Bristol-based Centre for Sustainable Energy.[46]

SOLAR CENTURY?

The sun's energy is the ultimate renewable, from an earthly perspective at any rate. Photovoltaic cells change sunlight into electricity. Cell efficiency improved in the '00s, from converting less than one eighth of the light falling on it into electricity, to converting almost a quarter. The cells are costly to manufacture, and have only a moderate lifespan of between 20 and 25 years, although there are hopes of lifespan extending to 40 years. No one really knows because only a small proportion of photovoltaic panels are more than ten years old. Cost is a barrier for households, especially those on low incomes. In 2014 a system with capacity of 4kWp – kilowatt peak, the maximum output under full solar radiation – was between about £5,800 and £7,400, according to advertisements.

Thermal solar systems are simpler, heating water used in the home or in commercial premises. Solar water heating systems need to be guarded from the risk of icing when air temperatures fall below freezing, and so solar power is really a more attractive option in tropical and semi-tropical low latitudes than in high-latitude regions like north-west Europe where direct sunlight is often lacking, especially during the long winters.

Renewables including solar made up 5.2% of the UK's energy consumption in 2013, compared with 4.2% in 2012.[47]The solar element of renewables was just 3.8% in 2013, a miniscule 0.2% of all the energy consumed. It is not yet a solar century.

Statistics reveal the deteriorating state of the UK's own energy production. In 2013 net imports accounted for 47% of all energy use, while during the two decades to 2004 in most years the UK was a net exporter of energy. In 2013, Russia supplied 41% of coal imports, Norway supplied 58% of gas imports and 40% of crude oil imports. Algeria, Saudi Arabia and other geopolitically challenged regions – or more accurately, corporations active in those nations – also have a big role in powering Britain.

On the face of it, the UK's energy use is falling, and in 2013 was 2% less than in 1970, when the population was 20% lower and the number of households was 29% less. The fall in energy consumption is partly due to efficiency savings, partly to price increases forcing people and organisations to economise deliberately, and also to national deindustrialisation.

SCHUMACHER'S LEGACY

Dr E F Schumacher originated the concept of 'Intermediate Technology' based on production using local labour and resources, production on a human scale in which individuals' efforts are recognised and valued. He argued that capital should serve communities, rather than the other way round, and he thought that if local communities were in control, they would protect their own environments and resources. His classic book, *Small is Beautiful: a Study of Economics as if People Mattered*,[48] inspired a following which continues today. The term 'Intermediate Technology' has been misunderstood as a stage between subsistence societies and the complex high-energy lifestyles of 'modern' people, but it means technology on a human scale, technology serving communities rather than controlling them.

The most reliable energy sources for the future will be local, and realisable on a small scale, as Schumacher envisaged. Local energy offers myriad combinations of benefits and drawbacks, but food production needs to depend on them to an increasing extent. Micro generation could become extremely important for British agriculture, as more farms adopt one or several of photovoltaic, wind and water-powered electricity, heat pumps for space heating, and biofuels to power agricultural vehicles and machinery.

Small-scale energy production, minimising the need for transport, and giving communities independent power supply, will increase resilience to outside shocks. But all this is a long way off.

Until then, we are likely to experience either tight energy supplies, or increasingly unsound financial systems which reduce demand for energy because people cannot afford to buy stuff, or phases of each scenario. As Gail Tverberg eloquently explains,[49] economies laden with excessive debt have to slash spending, or default. Whether demand collapses before supply or not, the result is the same and affects all sectors of the economy including vital ones like food production. Feeding plants to animals which process the plants into food for humans is a wasteful use of energy, so eating much less meat is a good idea, as long as the transition is carefully managed for livestock farmers and the meat industry. Here in the hills, a sudden collapse in livestock farming would cause severe economic distress.

DISTANCE BETWEEN THEORY AND PRACTICE

Rapid, forced adoption of a behaviour which seems at the moment to be highly desirable, such as a law for meat to be eaten much less often, is probably not a good idea at all, because expected and unexpected new problems will arise. Better to have a slower change, allowing time for industries and the public to readjust.

The practicalities of change are often under-estimated by evangelists committed to their cause. I know, for example, that ideally I should not use any fossil fuels, but I do.

Take a simple house. We are renovating a house which used to be a rural school. It has stone walls and a slate roof, and was built in 1875. Its life as a school was just 84 years, until 1959, when there were only a dozen pupils left. It was a cold, cold building. The school log books record that before the First World War, one small grate had to heat the whole building, which had a floor area of 760 square feet and a volume of 11,400 cubic feet, for the schoolroom was 15 feet high. Children who walked miles in the rain had nowhere to dry their clothes and were often sent home again. The damp interior was not good for children's health. Scarcely a week went by without someone suffering from a cold, cough, sore throat, chilblains, sickness, rash, or more serious ailment. The health and comfort of the children (and their teachers) was not a priority for the school inspectors of the 19th century or early 20th centuries. Not until 1926 did an inspector severely criticise the conditions in school. By then standards were improving almost everywhere, thanks largely to the growing social concern of local government officials and councillors.

When we acquired the building, it was still cold. A cylindrical wood-burning stove was the heat source in one living room, and the other relied on an open fire, onto which water trickled down the chimney every time it rained. The Rayburn in the kitchen could not be lit because the flue had collapsed. Now we have insulation 12 inches deep in the loft, a rebuilt and lined chimney, efficient double-glazed windows, and a re-slated roof.

In theory, to make the house warmer, we should insulate the ground floor, which has old red plain and patterned tiles on concrete. The conservation organisation English Heritage says, though, that "as a general rule, the excavation and replacement of significant solid ground floors should be avoided unless it is necessary to remedy a destructive defect",[50] and there is no such structural defect. The tiles are six inches by six, and hard to lift without breaking. If we lifted them, we would need a new hard floor covering. Instead, we decided to put timber floors over the tiles.

As for a heating system, the complicating factors include site restrictions, the capital cost and the feasibility of living with the recommended system. A wood-fired boiler, for example, uses entirely renewable fuel, but wood-fired boilers are like babies – you cannot go away and forget about feeding them. A wood-burning stove for supplementary heat is a different matter, and that will definitely go on the list. The timber source is our little wood. That's one of the benefits of a rural location, or the back of beyond, as city relatives tend to say.

As for whole-house heating, oil was out. Coal was out. I think liquefied petroleum gas should be out, but may be outvoted by other family members, who are used to LPG and like its convenience and its low carbon footprint compared with oil or coal.[51] I would have liked a domestic wind turbine, but the house is sheltered from strong winds. Solar photovoltaic panels and solar water heating looked more promising, although the best place for them would be on the roof slope facing the lane, and that conflicts both with planning guidance against placing panels on roof slopes facing roads, and our preference to keep the historical integrity of the slate roof.

135

We do not have any slopes facing south, although there is a possible spot in the back field, facing south-west down a narrow valley. With solar electricity and – vitally -- an electricity storage system, we could run night storage heaters, even if we were not connected to the National Grid. We could also consider an electric Aga which uses off-peak power. Agas are made of cast iron and can last for decades, and radiate heat like giant storage heaters.

Next step, a survey. Should we invite a Green Deal assessor? The Green Deal is confusing. I did not realise that the Green Deal and the Green Deal Home Improvement Fund are not identical, but the latter was a more generous branch of the former, although it did not include electricity from renewables. No surprise, therefore, that the Green Deal Home Improvement Fund, which offered cashbacks of up to £7,600 from the £450 million fund, ran out of money and closed on July 24th 2014 after less than seven weeks open, although the application process was bureaucratic and quite daunting. An additional £100 million was announced later in 2014.

The main Green Deal includes renewables and provides a loan to be repaid through electricity bills, and which is attached to the building, not to the occupier, so if the property is sold any remaining debt passes to the next occupier. Interest rates on the loans, typically 7.9% to 10.3% over 10 to 25 years,[52] are high in the context of the UK base rate of 0.5%, which at the time of writing had been in place since March 2009. To take part in the Green Deal, you have to engage suitably registered firms to assess your requirements, install the system and collect your repayments. There are a lot of strings.

Future resilience is one of the main purposes of improving energy efficiency in our former school. Three words fundamental to 'resilient' are 'renewable', 'diverse', and 'flexible'. The Green Deal requires you to install systems as recommended by the assessor, and the finance ties you in for as many years as you remain responsible for the property, so is not really flexible. The combination of systems we choose must be practical, convenient and as resilient as possible to future shocks. That means avoiding hyper-industrial technologies dependent on constant monitoring and needing energy-intensive maintenance.

Future resilience means paying close attention to the letters EROEI, energy return on energy invested in extraction, which is falling away. During the next decade, collapsing EROEI is going to land uncomfortably and noisily in the public arena, and force policy makers to confront it. If they delay, the option of step-by-step incremental change will disappear into the past.

---

[1] 'UK nuclear power plant gets go-ahead', BBC news business, October 21st 2013. www.bbc.co.uk/news/business-24604218

[2] The commission's policy areas were natural resources and climate change, consumption, housing and communities, economics, education, energy, health, local government, and transport. Food supply was not included.

[3] From section 3.3 in the Sustainable Development Commission's 2006 paper, *The Role of Nuclear Power in a Low Carbon Economy.*

[4] *The Energy Challenge,* from the Department of Trade and Industry, July 11th 2006.

[5] Nuclear Decommissioning Authority draft business plan 2014-17.

[6] The fissile isotope $uranium_{235}$ has a half-life of about 700 million years.

[7] Figures from the World Nuclear Association, December 2010.

[8] The slightly radioactive mineral thorium, which is about three times more plentiful than uranium, can absorb slow neutrons to breed $uranium_{233}$ for nuclear fuel. The fuel creation process is high cost, and there are technical difficulties with reprocessing, but India in particular has put thorium at the heart of its nuclear energy development programme. India has the world's second largest extractable reserves of thorium, 290,000 tonnes. Australia, with the most reserves, has about 300,000 tonnes.

[9] Wikipedia has an article on enriched uranium at http://en.wikipedia.org/wiki/Uranium_enrichment.

[10] 'South Carolina's nuclear-infused pork' by Josh Voorhees, www.slate.com/articles/news_and_politics/politics/2014/06/savannah_river_site_s_mox_project_why_is_the_government_spending_billions.html, June 4th 2014.

[11] 'Does nuclear power produce no CO_2?' by Dave Kimble, www.resilience.org/stories/2006-05-11/does-nuclear-power-produce-no-co2, May 11th 2006.

[12] Fast-breeder reactors produce more fuel than they consume for power generation.

[13] Pressurised water reactors use water to keep the reactor cool. This type of reactor is fuelled by uranium that is only slightly enriched.

[14] 'Nun sentenced to 35 months in prison for antinuclear peace protest', by Noelle Swan, The Christian Science Monitor, www.csmonitor.com/USA/USA-Update/2014/0218/Nun-sentenced-to-35-months-in-prison-for-antinuclear-peace-protest-video, February 18th 2014.

[15] See for example https://chernobyl-tour.com/about_us.html.

[16] The UK's newest reactor is a PWR at Sizewell B, which started generating electricity in 1996. All eight Magnox reactors were transferred from British Nuclear Fuels Ltd to the Nuclear Decommissioning Authority on April 1st 2005. Four Magnox rectors – two at Wylfa on Anglesey and two at Oldbury on the Severn estuary – were due to shut in 2010 but Wylfa was given an extension until December 2012 and a similar extension was granted for Oldbury. In 2015 Wylfa was the only Magnox station still operating in the UK.

[17] 'Extending the life of ageing nuclear reactors could help bridge the energy gap," by William Nuttall, EU Energy Policy Blog, www.energypolicyblog.com/2014/06/06/extending-the-life-of-ageing-nuclear-reactors-could-help-bridge-the-energy-gap/, June 6th 2014.

[18] 'Nuclear reactors will cost twice estimate, says E.ON chief', The Times, www.thetimes.co.uk/tto/business/industries/utilities/article2197468.ece, May 5th 2008.

[19] 'Assessing Fukushima damage without eyes on the inside' by Matthew Wald, New York Times, www.nytimes.com/2014/06/18/world/asia/measuring-damage-at-fukushima-without-eyes-on-the-inside.html?_r=0, June 17th 2014, and 'Japanese government signals restart of nuclear power plants' by Will Morrow, www.wsws.org/en/articles/2014/03/10/japa-m10.html, March 10th 2014.

[20] 'We are in denial about catastrophic risks', by Martin Rees, http://edge.org/response-detail/23864, 2013.

[21] Wikipedia has a useful article on nuclear fusion at http://en.wikipedia.org/wiki/Nuclear_fusion

[22] Figures from the World Coal Association, www.worldcoal.org/coal/uses-of-coal/

[23] Data from UK Coal, www.ukcoal.com/coal-around-the-world.

[24] This information came from the Uranium Information Centre, Melbourne, Australia, which promoted the nuclear industry worldwide until 2008. Nitrogen oxides include nitric oxide, nitrogen dioxide and nitrous oxide.

[25] 'EU green light for UK carbon capture and storage project' by Matt MgGrath, BBC News, www.bbc.co.uk/news/science-environment-27063796, April 7th 2014.

[26] 'E.ON shelves plans to build Kingsnorth coal plant' by Tim Webb, www.theguardian.com/environment/2010/oct/20/kingsnorth-coal, October 20th 2010.

[27] Special Report on Carbon Dioxide Capture and Storage, United Nations Intergovernmental Panel on Climate Change, 2005.

[28] 'Clean coal' technologies, carbon capture and sequestration, World Nuclear Association, www.world-nuclear.org/info/Energy-and-Environment/-Clean-Coal--Technologies/, April 2011.

[29] Thomas Gold died in 2004.

[30] 'The deep hot biosphere' is on pages 6045-6049, Proceedings of the National Academy of Sciences vol 89 no. 13, 1992. The 1999 book *The Deep Hot Biosphere* by Thomas Gold was published in New York by Springer.

[31] Abiogenic or abiotic theory refers to the production of a substance in the absence of living organisms.

[32] See 'Methane clathrate outgassing and anoxic expansion in Southeast Asian deeps due to global warming' by Pat Wilde and Mary S Quinby-Hunt, *Environmental Monitoring and Assessment* Vol.44 pps. 149-153, 1997.

[33] 'More bad news for fracking: IPCC warns methane traps much more heat than we thought' by Joe Romm, www.thinkprogress.org/climate/2013/10/02/2708911/fracking-ipcc-methane/ October 2nd 2013.

[34] Electrolysis is the process of obtaining a chemical decomposition reaction by passing electric current through a solution containing ions.

[35] When water is added to sodium borohydride, hydrogen is generated. Thus sodium borohydride is a solid storage medium for hydrogen. The vehicle manufacturer Chrysler trialled the 'Natrium' minivan, using sodium borohydride for a hydrogen fuel cell to give a range of 300 miles, but after the early 2000s the Natrium faded from the picture. The UK company Riversimple, founded by Hugo Spowers and based in the Powys, Wales town of Llandrindod Wells, is developing a small 'Network Electric' car with a low-power hydrogen fuel cell and a range of 300 miles. Sixty prototypes should be on the road in 2015. Honda had the FCX Clarity, launched at the Los Angeles Auto Show, California, in 2013, but this was discontinued in 2014 due to low take-up. Honda is reported to be developing a successor vehicle: www.dailytech.com/RIP+Honda+Insight+Fit+EV+and+FCX+Clarity+Killed+Due+to+Poor+Sales/article36304.htm. BMW launched a prototype fuel cell vehicle in 2010, and lent 100 to influential individuals. There are drawbacks to both hydrogen fuel cells and hydrogen combustion. For current news, see the Wikipedia article 'Hydrogen vehicle', http://en.wikipedia.org/wiki/Hydrogen_vehicle

[36] A free radical is an atom or group of atoms with at least one unpaired electron. Free radicals are unstable, easily reactive and can damage cells.

[37] Hydrocracking is a high-pressure, high-temperature refinery process to convert heavy black oil into petrol and diesel by cracking or breaking up larger molecules in the presence of hydrogen and a catalyst.

[38] 'Are hydrogen cars finally a reality?' by Barry Stevens, www.renewableenergyworld.com/rea/blog/post/2013/11/are-hydrogen-cars-finally-a-reality November 25th 2013.

[39] Figure from Paul Mobbs, slide 36 'Tidal', www.fraw.org.uk/ebo/tour_info/05_04-slides.html, not available directly in 2015 as site under revision.

[40] Reported in 'How it works: wave power station', BBC News, http://news.bbc.co.uk/1/hi/sci/tech/1032148.stm, November 20th 2000.

[41] Equivalent to a square almost 100 kilometres by 100 kilometres, or approximately 61 miles by 61 miles.

[42] NIMBY stands for 'not in my back yard'.

[43] Costs and benefits of on-farm digesters were explored in www.rase.org.uk/events/agri-science-events/AD_Walford-Mulliner.pdf, not available in 2015.

[44] The website www.uspowerpartners.org has a list of seven schemes in the USA that generate electricity from landfill methane, www.uspowerpartners.org/Topics/SECTION6Topic-LandfillMethane.htm.

[45] In January 2011. See www.energysavingtrust.org.uk/Generate-your-own-energy/Ground-source-heat-pumps

[46] www.cse.org.uk.

[47] Statistical press release, Digest of UK Energy Statistics 2014, July 31st 2014, Department of Energy and Climate Change.

[48] Published in Great Britain by Blond & Briggs Ltd, 1973.

[49] 'Low oil prices sign of a debt bubble', by Gail Tverberg, September 21st 2014, http://ourfiniteworld.com/2014/09/21/low-oil-prices-sign-of-a-debt-bubble-collapse-leading-to-the-end-of-oil-supply/

[50] Energy Efficiency and Historic Buildings: Insulating solid ground floors, English Heritage, March 2012

[51] LPG's Carbon Footprint Relative to Other Fuels, from Atlantic Consulting, 2009, www.aegpl.eu/media/21020/atlantic%20consulting%20scientific%20review%20carbon%20footprint,%20ed.%202009.pdf

[52] According to Which?, www.which.co.uk/energy/creating-an-energy-saving-home/guides/the-green-deal-explained/green-deal-finance---paying-for-the-green-deal/, accessed on October 17th 2014.

CHAPTER 7
TOMORROW'S SETTLEMENTS

CITYWORLD

The flow of migrants from country to city will, if unchecked, leave insufficient people to grow our food. Few policymakers see this as a problem, as they assume that farming will become more and more mechanised, and that synthetic fertilisers, herbicides and pesticides will carry on substituting for rotations, hoes and companion planting.

Villages far from cities are often ghettos of the elderly, who may be proficient in food production but whose skills die with them. The greying of the world's rural heartlands poses a huge question: should the long food supply chains ever rupture, for lack of fuel, water, soil, or any other essential input, there would be major trouble in the cities. The global population is expanding by some 81 million a year, while water and soil are depleting, and the supply of fuel for the whole urban superstructure is precarious.

A spate of TV programme about the 'real' Brazil, shown before the 2014 football World Cup kicked off in Sao Paulo, showed viewers shanty-town *favelas*, families gleaning rubbish for saleable recyclables, accompanied by guns, drugs and prostitution. Brazil is not a 'poor' country. The World Bank classes it as 'upper middle income' with GDP of US$2.253 trillion in 2012, $11,338 for each of the 198.7 million population. One of its big cities, Curitiba, home to 1.8 million people, is a famous exemplar of sustainable design, admired for its Bus Rapid Transit (BRT) network, its recycling rate of over 70%, its parks designed for leisure and to absorb floodwaters, its live-work homes, its encouragement for agriculture outside the city, and its city leaders' capacity for problem-solving.[1]

The world would need 45 new Curitibas every year just to house the extra population. China has a plan to meet the challenge, building what are called 'eco-cities' but which are planted in often inhospitable landscapes, and require long, energy-intensive supply lines. The building boom is no respecter of topography – at Lanzhou in Gansu province, north-west China, the plan is to flatten some 700 low mountains to create the space for a desert metropolis.[2]

One billion Chinese people are expected to live in cities by 2030, leaving only 300 million in the (much damaged) countryside. Unless there is land reform, there is little chance of farmers being able to feed the massive urban population. That is a major reason for Chinese organisations buying up arable land all over the world, including Brazil.

McKinsey & Company's Global Institute advocates concentrated cities in China, building over 7%-8% of arable land by 2030. Dispersed cities, McKinsey argued, would cover more than 20% of arable land over the same time span.[3] As China has only 7% of the world's arable land, just 0.09 of a hectare per person, there is scant scope to lose any more at all. Each year since 2000, about 0.7% of China's meagre total of arable land has been lost, much of it covered by factories and other industrial developments.[4]

Moran Zhang, reporting for the *International Business Times*, lists the ailments afflicting China's crop-growing land:

- One-fifth of it has polluted soils.
- Over-use of nitrogen fertilisers is turning land acidic.
- Farmers lack incentive to improve their land, because they have no rights over it. All land belongs to the state, and local governments derive more than a quarter of their revenues from land grabs – taking land from farmers and selling it to developers. Farmers are offered minimal compensation, about 2% of current market value, and with this they have to find new homes, new ways of making a living.[5] Disenfranchised farmers have little choice but to become city dwellers.[6]

Who will feed them? How? To rely on unfettered exports from countries in Latin America and Africa, where most of the 2.7 billion hectares which could be pressed into service for crop production are located, is surely unwise because of the negative consequences – loss of plants and wildlife in habitats currently rich, the adverse impact on climates of vegetation loss, rising demand for food from the local, fast-expanding populations, the energy costs of moving food around the world.

Ex-farmers will be living in Chinese cities, in homes currently empty – there are ghost blocks aplenty, the outcome of speculation – and in homes yet to be built, usually flats without gardens. Few planners appear to be paying attention to questions of sustainable food production, to the additional rural populations who will be essential for sustainable farming, or to the homes and supplementary livelihoods necessary for country dwellers. Even talking about a reversal of the migration to cities is often judged as quaintly old-fashioned, even Luddite, in China and everywhere else.

ONE PLANET WALES

Wales, as distinct from its neighbour England, is something of a trendsetter in rural policy. Wales has a One Planet Policy which has the potential to allow a new form of low-impact rural settlement, with food production at its heart. The name comes from the ambition for Wales, within a single generation, to use no more than its fair share of resources from our single planet. This is a big ask because population has accelerated away from resources, measured as 'global hectares' of biologically productive land and inshore fishing grounds. When 'One Wales One Planet' was envisaged back in the early 2000s, there were between 1.8 and 1.9 global hectares per person. In mid-2014, the share was only 1.55 hectares, but Wales was using some 4.8 hectares per person, a threefold overshoot.

Enthusiasts for the One Planet policy have set up the One Planet Council, which Jane Davidson launched into the world on May 17th 2014 at the Royal Welsh Spring Festival. Jane was the Welsh Government's Environment, Sustainability and Housing Minister between 2007 and 2011, when the One Wales One Planet policy was devised and adopted, and she moved on to lead the Institute for Sustainable Practice, Innovation and Resource Effectiveness (shortened to INSPIRE) at Trinity St David, University of Wales. The One Planet Council planned to launch training in 2015, for planners and applicants, to inform planners and help applicants cope with the bureaucratic demands of the planning system.

Planning regulations in England, even more so than in Wales, remain tightly drawn and hostile to new homes in the countryside – although farmers have been allowed to convert 'redundant' buildings into dwellings. The land question in England and Wales is the polar opposite of China. There, farmers have no rights, and can live on the land and produce food only for as long as the state allows. In England and Wales, most farmland is privately owned, and the state can acquire it from an unwilling seller only through a Compulsory Purchase Order. Britain is a small island, and England is the most densely populated part of it, with over 1,050 people per square mile overall, and 'countryside' is increasingly the preserve of the privileged. Wales has a lower population density, fewer than 385 per square mile, and a need for rural regeneration to which One Planet developments can and should contribute.

One Planet homes have to be made from recycled or sustainable new materials, sourced as locally as possible. They have to be unobtrusive, generate their own renewable electricity, and produce heat from renewable sources. The occupants have to devise and follow a management plan for at least 65% of their basic household needs to come from their land within five years.

The One Planet Council says that a "study of organic smallholding-type food production found the level of produce per annum to be 3.5 kg per square metre, equating to 35 tonnes per hectare. This is over 4 to 5 times greater than average UK wheat yields of around 7-8 tonnes per hectare on the best soil."[7] The idea is for occupants to produce most of their food, and also to build additional income streams, for example from holding training courses, doing artisan craft work, and selling surplus produce.

Intending One Planet homesteaders do need land, or capital to buy land, which restricts the number of applicants, but the first approval under the policy has been agreed.

SPENDING LESS IS PART OF THE ANSWER

Dan and Sarah Moody have a 16-acre smallholding[8] near Caerphilly in South Wales. They applied retrospectively for One Planet status, and received it, from Caerphilly Borough Council, in April 2014. They produce vegetables, fruit, eggs and meat, and in partnership with a charity called Kaleidoscope, teach rural skills to people recovering from alcohol and drug addiction. They have built a timber bungalow as an unobtrusive, low-impact dwelling.

To new applicants seeking planning permission under the One Planet policy, Sarah Moody offers two words of advice: "be patient".

"There are very few planning officers who have even heard of One Planet Development," she says, "but that will gradually change. Understandably they have a lot to get their heads around. We can't just think that because we are applying for an existing policy that everything will fit into the normal planning timeframe. In our case it took 13 months of waiting from the time that the application was submitted until we received our permission. We went to the planning committee twice. The first time, we appealed to the councillors to come out and have a look before they turned us down, and then we got a unanimous vote the second time around a few months later. Getting hot under the collar is not constructive and not good for one's blood pressure!"

There is tension between the government's ambitions for GDP growth and the One Planet aim to cut consumption of non-renewable resources. As Sarah says: "I know it's not what the government want us to do, but spending less is key. Spend less on buying stuff we don't need, which just ends up in landfill; spend less on fuel; invest in renewable energy -- our only household bill is £35 every four months! Spend less on food because you can grow your own. Growing food is great too because it's rewarding and more healthy. Spending less means you need to earn less to cover the costs. There are so many positives!"

FROM THE LAND AND BACK TO THE LAND

Environmental protection is core to the One Planet plan, urgently so, because as the London Zoological Society's Living Planet Index revealed, populations of more than 10,000 vertebrate species collapsed by more than half overall between 1970 and 2010. One Planet ventures specify more biodiversity, and no synthetic fertilisers, herbicides or pesticides. Water supply is from springs, streams and collected rainwater. Wastewater is processed on the land, with the nutrients reused to improve biodiversity and fertility. All biodegradable waste is composted, non-biodegradable waste is re-used and the aim is to have no rubbish sent off-site to landfill. As for transport, use of the private car is strictly limited, replaced by walking, cycling and public transport. To prove their reducing use of global hectares, One Planet dwellers have to log their resource footprints.

One Planet adopters are pioneers, and in the words of the One Planet Council:

> "Surplus food and other land based produce and crafts are sold locally to generate income, which reduces food miles by offering affordable, fresh, healthy food. Open days provide a way for people to see and experience examples of One Planet living. Educational courses bring people together to share skills and resources. Employment opportunities may arise from land based enterprises."[9]

By allowing One Planet ventures in the countryside, the Welsh Government is taking forward the work of 20th-century self-sufficiency guru John Seymour, who used to live on a smallholding in Pembrokeshire. The Moodys were inspired by John Seymour, whose work helped to keep rural and craft knowledge alive when the world around him was urbanising and globalising.

David Thorpe, a patron of the One Planet Council, offers a "blueprint for low-impact development" in his forward-looking book *The 'One Planet' Life*, published late in 2014.[10] *The 'One Planet' Life* is a compendium of practical information on how to establish and operate a low-impact land-based lifestyle, with 19 case studies, more than half of which are in Wales, the UK's hotbed of low-impact innovation. Smallholdings at the Lammas project feature prominently among the case studies.

THE LAMMAS PROJECT

The exciting Lammas eco-hamlet project was eventually given planning permission by Pembrokeshire County Council under its pioneer Policy 52, a forerunner of One Wales One Planet, despite strong opposition from within the council itself. Lammas is a community creating nine low-impact smallholdings at Glandŵr, near the Pembrokeshire-Carmarthenshire boundary.

The Lammas founders, orchestrated by Tao Paul Wimbush, sought to make this a legitimate rural development by obtaining planning permission before construction, rather than going ahead and then seeking retrospective permission. The exhausting process revealed the chasms that exist between policy and practice, and highlighted the clashing frames of reference which planners must somehow align.

The planning system in England and Wales is currently mired in the 1950s, when the global context was entirely different. Local food production was perceived as of diminishing importance because cheap transport meant imports could be sourced easily. 'The countryside' was a collection of landscapes for rich people to live in and for poorer people to enjoy from a distance. As for the poorer people, new jobs in the bright technological future would result in each generation being more prosperous than the last, and these new middle classes would be car-dependent and live in spacious suburbs.

A wave of New Towns, including Basildon, Bracknell and Harlow, reflected the Utopian aspirations of the Labour governments of 1945-50 and 1950-51, led by Clement Atlee. The first section of the M1 London to Birmingham motorway opened in November 1959. Dr Richard Beeching came along in the 1960s and on his recommendation the rural railway network was largely abandoned. He thought the car would rule from then onwards. The UK was still a manufacturing nation, jobs were plentiful, and when oil from British fields in the North Sea started flowing in the early 1970s, how bright the future seemed. The Franco-British supersonic Concorde made its first commercial flight in January 1976. The fatal flaw of Concorde, the fatal flaw of the transnational industrial age, was profligate use of energy. Concorde's engines burned 5,638 gallons of fuel per hour, or 563.8 gallons for every one of a capacity load of 100 passengers. Concorde was not sustainable, and was withdrawn from service in 2003, the final flight taking place on November 26th.

The England and Wales planning system, though, has remained in the 1950s, in a landscape of suburban estates, industrial 'parks' and town-centre bypasses.

Lammas's founders suffered years of failing to convince Pembrokeshire's planners and councillors of the legitimacy of their vision, because low-impact development was off the agenda when the Town and Country Planning Act 1947 was assembled, and has never been properly recognised as a permissible land use. We are stuck with outdated conceptions of development which oppress today's priorities for low-emission, low-energy, local lifestyles.

Battles over planning legislation since 1947 have focused on whether and how to tax the rise in land values following the granting of planning permission. The 1947 Act in Labour Britain introduced a 100% charge on the rise in land value, but the Conservatives suspended it when they came to power in 1951 and abolished it in 1954, although public bodies were able to buy land at its existing use value until 1959. The 1966-70 Labour government created both a Land Commission to buy land required for the implementation of national, regional and local plans, and a 'betterment levy' of 40% on value uplift. The following Conservative government of 1970-74 abolished both. When Labour returned in 1974, they tried a 'development land tax' of 80%, which Margaret Thatcher's first Conservative government of 1979-83 cut to 60%, before her second government did away with it in 1985. During the 'New Labour' interval between 1997 and 2010, a 'planning gain supplement' was mooted but the idea, vehemently opposed by developers, was dropped in 2007.

Since 1945 the big argument has been about taxing the financial gain conveyed by planning permission. The concept of land use for an ecologically balanced future is missing from the main legal framework.

The first gesture towards low-impact development was on the edge of the UK, in Pembrokeshire, West Wales. In June 2006 Pembrokeshire County Council and Pembrokeshire Coast National Park Authority (the planning authority in the national park) adopted Policy 52, Supplementary Planning Guidance 'Low Impact Development Making a Positive Contribution'.

Policy 52 applications must pass eight tests:

- There must be environmental, social and/or economic contribution with public benefit.
- All activities and structures must have low impact on the environment and low use of resources.
- If there are buildings on the site, their re-use must have been investigated and incorporated wherever practical.
- The project must be well integrated into the landscape and have no adverse visual effects.
- The project must require a countryside location, must involve agriculture, forestry and/or horticulture, and be tied directly to the land on which it is located.
- A sufficient livelihood for the residents on site must be provided.
- The number of adult residents should be directly related to the demands of running the enterprise.

- If the project involves members of more than one family, it must be managed and controlled by a trust, co-operative or other similar structure in which the occupiers have an interest.

The policy sets low-impact development firmly in a business frame. An appendix states that "if residents become unable to contribute to the proposal, due to age or illness, the Authorities will consider whether they can remain on the site". This condition implies that a low-impact settlement is only for the hale and hearty, and primarily an enterprise, not a home or group of homes.

Policy 52 became a Grand National course which the Lammas founders had to negotiate on two legs rather than four. The story unfolds in Tao Paul Wimbush's report 'The Process: Lammas' experience of the planning system December 2006-August 2009'.[11]

Tao Paul related how, in December 2006, the Lammas pioneers asked for a pre-application meeting with Pembrokeshire County Council's planning department. They had to wait until April 2007, when they met David Lawrence, head of planning, and Peter Sedgwick, forward planning officer and a co-author of Policy 52. At this meeting it was agreed that a conventional assessment of the agricultural viability of their proposed enterprises would not be appropriate, Tao Paul recalled.

Many hours of work went into preparing the 800 pages of documents and 200 drawings accompanying the planning application, which was submitted in quadruplicate in June 2007. All went quiet over the summer, and although the applicants requested a meeting with the head of planning, none was granted. Instead, according to Tao Paul's account, head of planning David Lawrence said he expected the plans to be recommended for approval.

In early October, five days before the planning committee was due to consider the application, the Lammas pioneers heard that the planning officer was advising refusal, citing insufficient data on traffic flows and inadequate business plans. They were not allowed to speak at the meeting. The application was turned down.

Page 148, line 14, 563.8 gallons should read 56.38 gallons

During the following six months, as reported in Tao Paul's account, the planning department refused to meet the applicants. The documents were rewritten, and by the time they were resubmitted in March 2008, they totalled 1,185 pages, over 250 scale drawings, more than 60 financial spreadsheets and two scale models.

Towards the end of May, case officer David Popplewell told the Lammas group that he wanted more time so he could send the application to ADAS, the privatised former state-owned Agricultural Development and Advisory Service. In the middle of August, Lammas applicant Nigel Lishman heard from ADAS's Aled Roberts that the business plan would be assessed against commercial agricultural criteria, with no reference to the ecologically-sympathetic permaculture they intended to practice. Meanwhile, 20 letters of support had been lost inside the planning department.

On September 9th, the revised application was refused. The Lammas business plan had been found wanting, mainly because ADAS had evaluated it against agribusiness criteria – contrary to the intentions of low-impact development in general and of Policy 52 in this particular case. Also, said Tao Paul, the officer's report to the planning committee contained a "plethora of structural and material errors".

The bureaucratic maze then became more complicated. The Lammas group tried to appeal, but the Planning Inspectorate said they could not, because the application which the committee had rejected for the second time had not been valid as it lacked an 'access statement'. However, Tao Paul and the rest of the Lammas group had been told by a council officer on March 11th that no 'access statement' was required. The Welsh Government said it could not intervene.

After two years of rebuffs, the Lammas applicants felt they had no option but to seek a judicial review. Just in time to prevent this from happening, Stephen Hurr, head of planning after David Lawrence, apologised for the error and promised that the planning

151

authority would return the application fee to the Lammas group. This was done, although not until April 2009.

A third planning application was handed into Pembrokeshire County Council on November 21st 2008. Once again case officer David Popplewell asked for more time, said Tao Paul Wimbush. The eight weeks, during which the application should have been decided, passed by. The applicants asked the Welsh Government to make the decision, because Pembrokeshire had failed to do so. The months passed until, on July 28th 2009, planning inspector Andrew Poulter held a public hearing, and the following day visited the site. He was accompanied by the case officer, who according to Tao Paul's report, had not previously ventured onto the land despite so many months of thinking about the proposal.

A month later, on August 27th 2009, the Lammas application was, at last, approved. The leader of Pembrokeshire County Council, farmer John Davies, called the decision a "dangerous precedent" – despite the fact that Policy 52 had been written by his own council and the Pembrokeshire Coast National Park Authority.

After 33 months of stress and dashed hopes, the Lammas project could begin.

As Larch Maxey, of Plymouth University's Centre for Sustainable Futures, has written:

"Lammas' softly-softly approach, seeking to work with the planning system, has led to huge delays while prospective residents living locally [have poured] savings into inadequate accommodation. Opportunities to harness people's energy have been lost. Whilst it remains invaluable to have the Low-Impact Development movement broadened by projects seeking planning permission before moving on, the planning system is ill equipped for the speed and scale of the challenges we face. Until it is equipped, people must continue to take direct action towards the sustainability transition in every way they can [including] building low impact lives."[12]

The British planning system is an enemy of direct action. Even when applicants for low-impact ventures ask for planning permission

152

before moving onto the land, as in the case of Lammas, planners and councillors who object to the concept have ways of stalling the plans. The Lammas project was in planning limbo for nearly three years, time which the applicants could never regain.

VISITING LAMMAS

Every Saturday morning in summer, there is a Lammas tour. On a drizzly Saturday in July 2014, I was among 15 or so, each paying £4. The money contributes to the income stream which has to come from the land, if the residents are to be allowed to stay there. The eco-village is on Tir y Gafel, 76 acres of former hill farm, near the hamlet of Glandŵr, close by the boundary with Carmarthenshire. Turning off the lane, we drove up a firm track through pasture to a parking area near the almost-completed hub building. I was surprised to find a parking area, but it is preferable to leaving cars in the narrow lane, or in the hamlet.

Melissa met us. She is young, like most of the Lammas group and unlike the norm in the rural fastnesses of West Wales, where to be over 65 is to be normal. "Seventeen adults and 16 children live here," she said, "and each family has between five and seven acres." There are nine smallholdings, occupying between two-thirds and three-quarters of the land, and there is also a lake and woodland managed communally. More than 12,000 trees have been planted since 2009, said Melissa, who led us towards her own holding. She lives in a wooden building which will eventually be the family's workshop. Their priority up till now has been developing their enterprises – bee keeping, weaving with willow, and seed production for a vegetable seeds company, as well as growing their own food and fuel. They must meet at least 75% of their household's needs from the land, within five years. This is even more demanding than the 65% required under the One Wales One Planet policy.

The hot dry summer had created a problem. The leat on the land contains a turbine which generates enough electricity for each

153

family to have between 2.5 and 2.8 kW, but when we visited there was too little water for the turbine to operate. As we can expect hotter, drier summers as an expression of climate change, this could become a repeating issue.

When the hydro turbine is functioning alongside the solar panels serving each household, there is often enough electricity to feed into the grid, if only there was a connection. There is no connection, because the planning permission requires the settlement to be independent of all utility services. Thus surplus electricity is wasted.

Melissa's home/workshop has straw bale walls clad with timber from Tir y Gafel's woodland. The roofing is Onduline, made from a baseboard of recycled cellulose fibres saturated with bitumen.

In many ways this smallholding reminded me of Ashmead, the Surrey smallholding on which my paternal grandparents lived for 25 years in the mid-20th century. Most of Ashmead was tree-covered, trees growing top fruit, the ground underneath grazed by poultry, and there were pigs too. Grandpa fed them waste food which he collected from hotels, a practice which was prohibited in the UK in 2001, an over-the-top response to that year's foot-and-mouth epidemic. The ban has never been lifted. Instead, in 2003, the EU applied the ban across member states.

Grandpa's smallholding was ecologically diverse. He was quite elderly, short of breath from the smoking which eventually killed him (I don't think I ever met a First World War veteran who did not smoke). He saw no sense in unnecessary work, and that included weeding for the sake of a tidy look.

My father grew vegetables to supply London markets and local retailers. He liked weed-free fields and hoed mechanically and at ferocious speed by hand, but he left field margins alone. Dad was not keen on trees, though, believing that they reduced crop yields by shading out sunlight.

Tir y Gafel is more like Ashmead than Redlands, my mother and father's farm, but the smallholders are not behind the times. They are, rather, ahead of the times because they have chosen permaculture, a form of farming which replicates natural diversity and is based on ecosystems. There are no areas of mono-cropping. Instead, crops are planted in small blocks, using principles of companion planting, juxtaposing different plants which protect each other from pests, or which have other symbiotic advantages.

Melissa handed us over to Hoppi, who has two Jersey cows which between them yield up to 24 litres of milk a day. On sloping land above the track leading to their barn and temporary home, Hoppi pointed out cob and hazel nut trees, and blueberries backed by larch trees. "Voles were eating some blueberry roots," said Hoppi, "so we put chickens in there to scratch at the grass and expose the vole runs. Owls preyed on the voles, so they did less damage – but the chickens ate the blueberries!"

Hoppi's husband, the Lammas pioneer Tao Paul Wimbush, did huge quantities of work to guide the Lammas project through the convoluted planning process, and is now an energetic smallholder. The Wimbush family are, like Melissa, living in what will be their workshop. They have not built their house yet because their energies have gone into creating their smallholding. When the house is up, the whole workshop will be available for the dairy, vegetable store, woodworking shop and kitchen for preparing Hoppi's organic skin care products.

A commercial farm would have been out of reach for Hoppi and Tao Paul. A 999-year lease for the smallholding plot cost £35,000, paid to the Industrial and Provident Society which owns the freehold. The Ecology Building Society supported them with a £22,500 mortgage.. Their timber barn, hay store and cow house cost just £3,500 to build, with the roof the most expensive part.

The Wimbushes have excavated a reservoir, put up a polytunnel for high-value crops, and created a vegetable garden rich in crops from around the world. Their ducks snaffle the slugs, besides providing eggs and occasional meat.

"There's more uncultivated land than I expected to see," said one of our group as the visit drew to a close. They would probably have said the same about Ashmead, or my garden come to that, but the food and fuel crops are dispersed, interplanted, naturalistic, not corralled into uniformity.

There's a message here for the planning system, which reinforces old settlement patterns and too often prevents low-impact proposals from inspired individuals. Policy-makers and planners tend to pigeon-hole knowledge about low-impact development as 'quaintly old-fashioned' or even 'archaic' and accord to it a lower value than knowledge about current technologies. A post on 'West Wales News Review' considered this barrier:

Low Impact Development Hampered by 'Illegitimate' Knowledge

"The mine of information that is www.lammas.org.uk, the website for the Lammas eco-village project at Glandwr, Pembrokeshire, has a section full of research reports, all fascinating, but one appealed to me particularly, because it dealt with our understandings of 'knowledge', and that was a topic of my own PhD thesis several years ago.

Knowledge which is officially valued influences public policy far more than knowledge which is perceived as 'common' or non-expert. This is a conclusion of Karolina Rietzler, in her 2012 M.Sc thesis for the Albert Ludwigs Universität, Freiburg. Karolina, studying in the environmental governance department, titled her thesis 'The Role of Scientific Knowledge and Other Knowledge Types in Grassroots Sustainability Initiatives: an exploratory case study of a low impact development eco-village in Wales'. The issues she highlights go a long way to explaining the reluctance of governments to treat low-impact development as anything other than a niche, and the reluctance of local planning authorities to depart from the 'scientific' assessments to which they have become accustomed.

In Karolina's analysis, a key insight of German sociologist Ulrich Beck has been lost on mainstream policy makers. He argued that the environmental crisis should be understood as a "profound institutional crisis of industrial society itself".[13] If this is the case, industrial society cannot be both the cause of and cure for the crisis. Yet policymakers and policy implementers tend to "dismiss knowledge and understanding generated outside accredited scientific institutions".[14] Those institutions have been the fount of knowledge for the failing (or failed) industrial society.

For Karolina, the Lammas project of nine smallholdings at Tir y Gafel, Glandŵr, represents transdisciplinary research, which is often discounted by policymakers because it does not come from a defined scientific tradition. The same policymakers fail to appreciate that 'subjects' and 'disciplines' are human constructions, and that knowledge is unitary. Instead, they are guided by the "legitimating function of scientific knowledge from recognized sources".[15]

At Lammas, Karolina found new knowledge being created by citizen scientists, with different skills, co-operating with other, but planners tend not to regard this knowledge as 'legitimate', because it has not been produced by people they regard as 'experts'.

The requirement for 'experts' disadvantages low-impact development because proponents usually cannot afford to hire them. Low impact means low cash, too. The generation of a large cash surplus is not on the low-impact agenda, but for 'experts' to be afforded, there needs to be a plentiful source of money. Low-impact applicants start with their hands tied behind their backs, and no one comes along to untie them. This means that, although paying lip service to the desirability of low-impact living, policy makers ensure it rarely happens because of the ways they nobble the pioneers.

published July 5th 2014 in 'West Wales News Review' as 'Low Impact Development Hampered by 'Illegitimate' Knowledge'

The concept of low-impact development is also hard for many policymakers to accept because the associated lifestyles are somewhat different from the modern expectation/aspiration of mortgage, commute, shopping and foreign holidays. Low-impact lives are less connected to the money economy, and this is a threatening prospect for those powerful people whose prosperity depends on the public spending as much as possible.

Tipi Valley as Diffusion Centre

Tipi Valley is not paradise – too cool and rainy – but people can live there quietly and with very little money. Tipi Valley is a Carmarthenshire low-impact village, founded in 1974 with no permission at all, and the subject of protracted battles with the planning authority, Carmarthenshire County Council. The community describes itself thus, on the alternative communities 'Diggers and Dreamers' website, www.diggersanddreamers.org. uk :

> "To be honest, we're a bunch of hippies, some of us 'originals'. Tipi Valley is high in the Welsh hills, on 200 acres that we have bought bit by bit over 35 years. Our oldest land has already reverted to temperate rainforest. The idea is that we are part of nature, living within nature. Thus all our homes are low-impact dwellings such as tipis, yurts, domes and thatched or turf-roofed round houses. We are a village, not a commune, and everyone is responsible for their own economy. We do not have regular business meetings, and we never vote. It works by consensus and personal relationships."

Forty years on, Tipi Valley is no longer 'separate'. Children who grew up in the valley often live more energy-intensive lives than their parents, but possess practical skills which set them apart from children who were raised in houses and who received a conventional, book-based education. They can also support themselves and their families in unpromising surroundings because they have experience of getting by on very little.

These Tipi Valley 'graduates' frequently live in houses themselves, but like to stay close to the valley. They are electricians, carpenters, plumbers, plasterers, growers, therapists, often more than one at a time. They socialise and they help each other out, and they are also a bridge between the valley and the surrounding communities. Their parents were much more often English middle-class rebels than Welsh country folk, but several now have a foot in both groups. The original 'back to Nature' purpose of Tipi Valley's founders no longer guides many in the second and third generations, at least not so strongly, but as they integrate into other communities, they bring a rich range of different perspectives. If the founders had not battled for permission to stay, and had meekly left, the story of their experiences, including the capability to adapt to the environment, would be missing.

FAYE'S STORY

The Tipi Valley community has a committed nucleus and a more temporary periphery. Faye and her parents and brother were frequent visitors there, and so not entirely peripheral but not in the nucleus either, from the time Faye was eight until she was 14, when she moved to live in the valley permanently with her best friend and best friend's mother.

"When I was seven my mother decided to take us out of school," said Faye. "It was OK for a while – my mum was a qualified teacher – but mum and dad soon decided to go travelling. The whole summer when I was eight we spent in Tipi Valley. We kids were outside most of the time, riding bikes, making dens and go-karts. We weren't there in the winter much, because the conditions could be very harsh. If you hadn't collected wood you didn't have a fire and couldn't cook. If you didn't walk across the fields to the stream you didn't have water, unless we had snow and you melted it. There was no electricity, no gas, no piped water, no drains, no bus service. There used to be a shop in a caravan, selling whole foods, and there was a library – a wooden shed in which people left books, all kinds of books, and that was one of my favourite places."

After six years of an itinerant life, and becoming more and more uneasy about her missing education, Faye left her own family to return to the valley, live in a caravan and start school again. "I was put with pupils a year younger, and in a special needs class," Faye remembered. "I had missed more than six years of education, and seven years of school, and was desperate to catch up. It was quite an effort to attend school regularly. We left at 7.30 in the morning to walk up the hill and wait for the taxi which took us to the school bus stop in Abergorlech village. The journey was over ten miles each way, and not at all straightforward. We rarely got home again much before 5.30."

At the time, many parents living in Tipi Valley were dismissive of education and did not send their children to school. Who were these parents? Some, those most likely to live in tipis, were trialling an alternative lifestyle separate from the established community in the area. They grew their own food, made strict regulations about land use, and totally prohibited loose dogs. The caravan dwellers, on a different part of the site, were more likely to be refugees from a society which they found uncongenial or hostile.

Did anything unite these groups? "They were all non-materialistic," said Faye. "Possessions did not matter. Also, there was a real sense of community. People trusted each other and maybe mistrusted people living outside the valley."

They were consuming much, much less than people living in houses. "It was hard to go shopping," said Faye. "If someone had a car or van, they might take a group to town once a week or fortnight. Most people didn't have much money anyway. I can't think of anyone who had a conventional job or who worked in an office."

That did not mean valley people were idle. They grew plants of all sorts, gardened for clients, made and sold arts and crafts, did casual work. Those who opted for maximum self-sufficiency worked extremely hard at surviving.

For Faye's parents, conventional education was unimportant. She has a totally different view and although she missed out on seven years of school, she worked to support herself through studying for GCSEs and A levels at college, and a law degree at university. Has this achievement distanced her from her childhood friends in Tipi Valley? No, she says, they remain friends, and many are close friends.

The first generation of children from Tipi Valley, those born in the 1970s and 1980s, generally live differently from their parents. Most opt for mod cons like electricity and running water, and they support themselves and their families with skills they have learnt. They send their children to school, and this is an important way in which their lives are different from their parents. They have integrated into the communities in which they live, and in the process they bring change – more concern for self-reliance and for protecting their environment, and at the same time a willingness to challenge officialdom in all its guises. Faye's own career reflects a wish to put people first, working as she does for Citizens Advice as operational services manager for the Swansea Neath Port Talbot region.

BEN'S STORY

Ben was a year old when he moved into Tipi Valley with his mother, and he moved to live outside when he was 22. He learned to survive, to make what he needed from what was at hand. Every day as a child it was his job to fetch water, half a mile there and half a mile back. When he was 12 he moved out of the tipi he shared with his mum and her partner, with whom he did not get on, into a small tipi which was his 12th birthday present. Every Wednesday he was given money to travel to Carmarthen, about 20 miles, and buy food to cook for himself.

Life was punctuated by trips to Greenham Common Women's Peace Camp, to Stonehenge, and to festivals. Ben did not go to school.

"When I was 14 I got really worried about missing school," he said. "I went to the comprehensive school in Llandeilo and they let me in but I was put in a special needs class with younger children. I didn't tell anyone I was from the valley for a long time."

Plenty of signs in Llandeilo showed Ben that people from the valley were not welcome. "There were places like cafes with signs saying 'No Hippies', he remembered. "Town was a scary place."

Ben learned quickly at school, and was admitted to the sixth form. "I'd been channelled into Leisure and Tourism, but I really didn't want to do that," he said. He left and did a number of labouring jobs, qualified as a fork lift driver then as a heavy goods driver, and drove lorries all over Britain for a few years. Now in his mid-30s, he is in his third year at university, working for a degree in live event technology.

"I much prefer my life now," he says. "I say put education first, education is vital, and everyone should have the opportunity to go to school. I think all my friends from the valley who now have children all say the same, they all make sure their children go to school." Those friends are in many ways a family, as they have remained close over the years. They depended on each other when they were children, and that continues.

"A lot of the parents who lived in the valley were rebelling," said Ben. "They were running away from their parents' expectations, but they imposed that rebellion on us too."

The years out of school were not lost years. Ben is intensely practical. He is a carpenter with flair, he is a clever cook, he knows which wild plants are safe to eat and which are not, he knows how to grow his own food. He has inherited land in the valley which he intends to keep. "I think it's different there now," he said. "Relations with local farmers are better, several will stop and chat. It used to be temporary visitors with dogs who created most of the problems, because the dogs would chase sheep, but most of the people living in the valley now have settled there."

The skills learned by children in the valley, mostly by trial and error, are necessary in the coming world of greater self-reliance. Mainstream culture nowadays defers too much to Health and Safety, and mollycoddles children in many ways, while subjecting them to stress in others, such as repeated testing in school. The children of the counter-culture have practical skills which should not be under-valued, because they are vital to survival in difficult times.

RURAL EXCLUSION

The Wales-launched One Planet Council represents low-impact development pioneers, many of whom have in turn been inspired by people such as the Sussex woodsman Ben Law, whose hand-built cruck-frame roundwood-timber home has featured on Kevin McCloud's Channel 4 series *Grand Designs*. The planners, when they eventually allowed construction, insisted that occupancy is tied to Ben himself. This means the home cannot be sold, and also that unless the tie is lifted, if Ben left it would have to be demolished.

Planning laws seem to work in particularly perverse ways. The aim, to prevent open countryside from burial under concrete, is sound enough, but they function like the Inclosure Acts in that they favour influential groups, such as the volume house builders nowadays, and marginalise individuals who want to live on a small area of land and make a small living from it. The Inclosure Acts, which privatised common lands in England, Wales, Scotland and Ireland and which reached a crescendo in the 18th and 19th centuries, transferred land rights away from communities and into the hands of influential landowners, a process which history suggests is checked only through the intervention of revolutions.

The Labour Land Campaign estimated that in the early 21st century, 189,000 families owned two-thirds of the UK's land. The 40,000 with the greatest landholdings had title to about half. Consider that the population of the 'United Kingdom' reached 64.1 million in mid-2013. If we take the average household size as 2.35 persons, we have approximately 27.28 million separate households. The 40,000 are only 0.1466% of this total, one household in every 682 owning half the UK's land. The cost of land is beyond the reach of the great majority of people, and Inheritance Tax exemptions assist landowning families to keep land assets in the family, thereby reinforcing the divide between landowners and the landless.

Planning laws also make exemptions for new country houses of architectural excellence. England's Paragraph 55 of the National Planning Policy Framework allows such departures from the norm of no new building in open countryside. Like Inheritance Tax exemptions, Paragraph 55 is for those able to risk many tens of thousands of £s in design fees for a project that might not be approved. Paragraph 55 is not for self-sufficiency enthusiasts of the kind who look to Lammas.

Living in the countryside, working on one's own land and deriving a living from it, is such a fundamental element of a 'property owning democracy' that its withering away calls for more interrogation. Enter Simon Fairlie, editor of *The Land* and mastermind behind Chapter 7, an organisation which gives planning advice to smallholders and other actual and aspiring country-dwellers who seek to work on and with the land.

Access to land should be widely attainable by those who wish to work on it, Simon believes. In overcrowded England, ownership in few hands, and the relative ease with which land can be transferred down the generations, combine to exclude newcomers unless they are remarkably wealthy. For new rich landowners, their acres are often a protective barrier between them and the world outside.

According to Savills,[16] the average price of prime arable land in Great Britain rose 9.8% in the first half of 2014 and only in Wales and Scotland was the average price less than £8,000 per acre, in Scotland barely so. Top grade 1 land changed hands at over £12,000 per acre. Cash was the main source of funds in 80% of sales. This is a startling statistic, showing that LAND IS PURCHASED BY THE ALREADY WEALTHY.

Over the first six months of 2014, even the price of poor grassland was on the rise, up 5.7% across Great Britain. Savills attributes this to the booming market for country homes.

Land prices are out of all proportion to its income-generating capacity. Land is an asset class. Given governments' refusal to redistribute land wealth, for aspiring new entrants to farming who lack family land the only ways in are courtesy of philanthropic landlords who are prepared to sell or rent cheaply. The Landshare scheme launched by Hugh Fearnley-Whittingstall in 2009 was a promising step in this direction, and by September 2014 had attracted over 74,000 members either seeking growers for under-used plots or plots to grow on. Matches are initiated by the website www.landshare.net, which is not well served by its mapping software (the site told me I am not in the UK, no matter which postcode or town name I entered, with spaces or without). Landshare is a great idea for people who want to collaborate with others near their homes, on a season-by-season basis, but it is not a route into living on the land.

Politicians mostly ignore issues of food security unless faced with a crisis. The National Farmers' Union lobbies politicians, but on behalf of larger producers. County councils used to provide large numbers of smallholdings for rent, but have sold most of them off in the belief that big businesses are the future. In 1966 there were 12,882 local authority smallholdings in England, but in 2012-13, only 2,836. In the year 2012-13, county councils disposed of much more land, 1,183 hectares, than they acquired, 129 hectares, although the holdings provided a total operational surplus of £13.325 million, an average of almost £4,699 each. New tenancies totalled 123, but tenancies terminated amounted to 211.[17]

The Tenant Farmers Association (TFA) lobbies for local authorities to reverse the disposal of their smallholdings estates:

"County Council smallholding estates should be valued by individual local authorities and the nation as a whole as vital to the sustainability of providing a viable entry point and ongoing development for those seeking a career in agriculture."[18]

This suggestion is one of many in the TFA's report *2020 Vision for Agriculture*, sponsored by solicitors and parliamentary agents Bircham Dyson Bell and published in August 2010. The TFA, keen for many more agricultural tenancies to be made available to new entrants, draws attention to a barrier at the end of working life, the lack of housing for tenant farmers who wish to or need to retire. Too often there is nowhere for them to go. The TFA proposes tax incentives for landlords to provide housing, and also an end to the removal of agricultural restrictions on dwellings, while at the same time advocating permission for rural workers to live in homes with agricultural ties.

Organisations for small-scale farmers, owners and tenants, include the Landworkers' Alliance, which in April 2014 demonstrated in London outside DEFRA, the Department for Environment, Food and Rural Affairs, to protest about the marginalisation of small farms. The Alliance is linked to the international movement for small-scale farmers, La Via Campesina.

Despite all the lobbying, governments are reluctant to prioritise smallholding, small farming, peasant farming, call it what you will. The big corporations have more money and clout and can buy the most expensive advice. No wonder that many intending smallholders have decided to take their futures into their own hands and to raise money outside conventional sources. In 2014 the Biodynamic Land Trust Community Benefit Society, directed by Martin Large, is in the process of buying Week Farm, Totnes, with the proceeds of a community share offer.

Totnes in Devon is a hub of rural revival, the stomping ground of Transition Towns guru and founder member Rob Hopkins, and close by Schumacher College, a centre for sustainability courses and the first college in the world to offer an MA in the Economics of Transition, validated by the University of Plymouth. Totnes attracts transition enthusiasts from all over the place, but the magnetism of the place has a perverse impact, a real downside for local people. The property market has soared away from the resources of people in the great majority of local jobs. The website Rightmove was offering, in September 2014, two-bedroom flats and small three-bedroomed terraced homes mainly for £200,000 and above. What about a detached? Forget it unless you have in excess of £300,000.

Yet of the 23,000 or so jobs in the Totnes parliamentary constituency, 9,000 were in 2013 filled by women working part-time, for a median gross weekly wage of £136.20, a grand annual total of £7,082.40, if they had a job all year. Forty per cent of these part-time jobs paid £119.50 a week or less. The 6,000 jobs filled by women working full-time paid a median £467, £24,284 a year. A typical two-bedroom flat would be over eight times this wage. The situation is worse for the 8,000 full-time jobs done by men, with median weekly gross income of £462.80, £24,065 a year, which is less than the wage for full-time women.[19]

Totnes is fashionable, largely thanks to its status as a star Transition Town. That star status has not transformed the low-wage economy, but it has pushed property prices skywards as independent professionals and the well-heeled retired move in. Totnes, and other 'green' transition towns and villages such as Stroud in Gloucestershire, and Lewes and Forest Row in East Sussex, are prosperous places with green reputations which add to their exclusivity and thus to the costs of living there.

Aware of the paradox, Transition Totnes is trying to take some corrective action. The group has set up the Transition Homes Community Land Trust with the objective of building 25 'affordable' homes on a seven-acre site, purchased with £250,000 lent by members of the public. This would be a low-impact development, including land for allotments, coppicing, and for a community hub building. The homes, for shared ownership or renting, would be for local people in need of housing, and unable to buy or rent on the open market. At the time of writing in spring 2015, there was no planning permission for the site, which is not in a zone scheduled for development.

The UK's national housing shortage -- exacerbated by an excess of immigrants over emigrants of 260,000 in the 12 months to June 30th 2014, and over 250,000 in each of six separate years between 2000 and 2014[20] -- prompts calls to build on Green Belts, especially around London, the golden city. Yet in the village I live in, deep in West Wales, I look over the road to a terrace of eight homes, three of which are empty – one abandoned, one for sale, one a rarely-used holiday home. Vacant houses are scattered all around the village. There are too few jobs within easy commuting distance, and very few well-paid jobs. This great divide between South East England and most of the rest of the United Kingdom is a threat to social cohesion, and therefore to future political stability. The planning regulations which treat the countryside as protected landscapes (and all but outlaw new developments except for privileged people who live there already) inhibit the creation of new rural communities and, instead, function as a funnel into energy-intensive urban living. One Planet developments in Wales are early steps in a counter-movement towards sustainable future settlements, but a marathon remains to be run.

---

[1] It's ironic, though, that manufacture of vehicles and vehicle parts is a key element of Curitiba's economic base. German, Japanese, French and Chinese auto firms have chosen the city as a base. The young, dynamic workforce is an attraction for manufacturers and good for city finances, because these are taxpayers. Only 6% of Curitibans are aged 65+! Information from the Brookings Institution, 'Curitiba metropolitan area profile'; 'Sing a song of sustainable cities', TED (Technology, Entertainment and Design) talk by former city mayor Jaime Lerner; and slides at www.slideshare.net/mrcornish/sustainable-curitiba.

[2] 'China to flatten 700 mountains for new metropolis in the desert', by Jonathan Kaiman, www.theguardian.com/world/2012/dec/06/china-flatten-mountain-lanzhou-new-area, December 6th 2012.

[3] 'Preparing for China's urban billion', McKinsey Global Institute, March 2009.

[4] P.104 in *Countering 21st Century Social-Environmental Threats to Growing Global Populations*, by Frederic R Siegel, Springer Briefs in Environmental Science, 2015.

[5] '7 reasons why you don't want to be a farmer in China' by Moran Zhang, www.ibtimes.com/field-dreams-7-reasons-why-you-dont-want-be-farmer-china-1394965, August 22nd 2013.

[6] City dwellers have to cope with great pollution challenges of their own. In Lanzhou, 2.4 million people were told not to drink the tap water in June 2014. It was contaminated with benzene. Source: Xinhua News Agency, June 12th 2014.

[7] One Planet Council, www.oneplanetcouncil.org.uk/about/

[8] Nant-y-Cwm has a Facebook page, https://www.facebook.com/NantYCwmFarm.

[9] www.oneplanetcouncil.org.uk/12goodreasons/

[10] *The 'One Planet' Life: a Blueprint for Low Impact Development*, by David Thorpe, Routledge, dated 2015.

[11] www.lammas.org.uk/oldsite/lowimpact/documents/TheProcess_000.pdf

[12] See 'Lammas Ecovillage Wales gets planning approval (finally!)', earthfirst.org.uk/actionreports/node/23012

[13]Ulrich Beck, Anthony Giddens and Scott Lash, *Reflexive Modernization: Politics, Tradition and Aesthetics in the Modern Social Order*, Blackwell Publishers, Oxford, 1994.

[14] Alan Irwin, *Citizen Science: a study of people, expertise and sustainable development*, London, New York: Routledge, 1995, pps.67-68.

[15] Karolina Rietzler, www.lammas.org.uk/oldsite/lowimpact/documents/ThesisKarolinaRietzler2012.pdf, 2012, p.68.

[16] *Market in Minutes, Q2 Farmland Market*, July 2014, from Savills.

[17] *Sixty-third Annual Report to Parliament on Smallholdings in England 1 April 2012- 31 March 2013*, published by DEFRA, February 2014.

[18] www.tfa.org.uk/wp-content/uploads/2013/03/TFA2002 VisionforAgricultureV7LoRes.pdf

[19] *Annual Survey of Hours and Earnings 2013*, provisional figures from ONS, table 10.1a, gross weekly pay by parliamentary constituency.

[20] Data from Migration Watch, www.migrationwatchuk.org/latest-immigration-statistics

CHAPTER 8
THROUGH THE POLITICAL MIASMA

THE AGRARIAN FUTURE

Life in Britain in 2050: what might it be like? Energy use may have fallen by two thirds. People will spend more time carrying out the activities necessary for survival – finding and growing food, preparing it, storing it, cooking it -- so there will be less time for 'careers' or for 'leisure'. Repair skills will be in demand. People will mend anything and everything, as long as they can get hold of suitable materials. The age of long-distance commuting will have ended, and long-haul holidays will be distant memories.

At least half the working population would need to work on the land. Fewer people would earn enough to pay income tax, and so government would struggle to fund public services like health, education, social security and defence. The degree of occupational specialisation that characterised the 20th century would not be possible if half the population were engaged in the production of necessities. The role of women would change, in fact society could revert to a more traditional patriarchal system because women have benefited hugely from job opportunities in the public sector, and thus will suffer disproportionately as publicly-funded work declines.

We tend to assume that the future will be an enriched version of the past, although this rosy expectation has been somewhat dashed in the UK by the fall in real wages since 2007-08.[1] The nation remains highly popular with wealthy incomers because of its (publicly funded) police force, defence, education and health services, with the result that large numbers of the indigenous population cannot compete with moneyed incomers for land and

171

property. There is nothing new in this, as our colonial past testifies, and it is revealing to view incoming purchasers through the eyes of the colonised, rather than those of colonisers. Within the UK, inhabitants of National Parks and pretty seaside resorts have long experience of being outbid in land and property markets.

Land in the UK, and over most of the privatised world, is regarded as an individual asset much more than as a communal one, and often as an asset to be exploited to the full. Worrying research from Sheffield University indicates that soils in the UK's farming areas have been alarmingly depleted of nutrients, and are likely to offer no more than 100 more harvests. The researchers -- Jill Edmondson, Zoe Davies, Kevin Gaston and Jonathan Leake[2] -- found that soils on urban allotments are much less compacted and more fertile than today's rural soils, with 32% more organic carbon, and carbon to nitrogen ratios 36% higher.

Economic pressures – and desires to maximise short-term returns – have led many farmers to mine their soils and to short-circuit processes of replenishment by adding high concentrations of nitrogen, phosphates, potassium and other minerals, in a similar method of nutrition to a fast-food chain selling quick calories. The pernicious effects were clear by 1970, when Michael Blake wrote *Down to Earth: Real principles for fertiliser practice*.[3] He wrote:

"…how many farmers appreciate that to feed plants with pure and highly soluble concentrated salts (as now provided) is the complete antithesis of Nature's evolved method of plant nutrition by slow release of soil minerals. The complementary measures necessary when using large amounts of these concentrated salts must be carefully considered, and constitute a vital part of the farm fertilising plan.

"A fertile soil is the natural end product of the activity that goes on above and within the surface layer. The soil population (including the plant roots) creates productivity by transforming radiant energy from the sun into chemical energy by photosynthesis and heat absorption by the plant. Plant material so produced becomes the energy source for animal and microbial life. Within the surface much physical energy is expended by all species in securing its standard of living. Thus a mole or a worm burrowing or making excrement, a seed germinating, or a root growing; energy is being expended in moving soil. Such incessant movement by countless organisms making their habitat compresses and distorts the soil mass creating a structure in which all species can breathe, eat, and drink. In short, a fertile soil."

 -- *Down to Earth* p.4

Monocultures destroy the complexity which is crucial for soil health. If only everyone had taken Arthur Fallowfield seriously! Arthur, played by Kenneth Williams, was a country character on the 1958-1964 BBC radio series *Beyond Our Ken*, starring Kenneth Horne. Arthur's answer to every question began "Well, I think the answer lies in the soil".

Sheffield University's Nigel Dunnett, professor of planting design and vegetation technology, is quoted in *The Independent*[4] as saying:

"With a growing population to feed, and the nutrients in our soil in sharp decline, we may soon see an agricultural crisis.

"Meanwhile we are also seeing a sharp decrease in bio-diversity in the UK which has a disastrous knock-on effect on our wildlife. Lack of pollinators means reduction in food."

Professor Dunnett, echoing the findings of Jill Edmondson and her colleagues, believes that cities, with their allotments on soils that are often more fertile than farmland, must become centres of food production. What a shame that so few allotments are left.

ALLOTMENTS ALERT

The popularity of the British allotment, a field divided into plots on which individuals can grow fruit and vegetables, declined in the decades after the Second World War, as imported food became plentiful and cheap. People preferred to buy holidays and leisure activities rather than spend their days off digging and weeding.

Local councils, which owned much of the national allotments estate, sold them off. During the food-shortage years of the Second World War, there were some 1.4 million allotment plots in England and Wales. By the 21st century, the total had collapsed to 250,000 plots.

In 2002, though, allotments began a revival, with funding for the Allotments Regeneration Initiative from the Esmée Fairbairn [5] Foundation and the Tudor Trust. The initiative ended in 2012, after distributing over £652,000 in grants to 132 projects.

British allotments are usually measured by the 'rod', which is either a length of 5.5 yards, or an area of 30.25 square yards.[6] The typical allotment is between five and ten rods, around 150 to 300 square yards, between one thirty-third and one seventeenth of an acre.[7] One individual would need between three and five allotments to feed themselves on a vegan diet, and a diet with meat like beef and lamb would require twenty times more land, 60 to 100 allotment plots, to feed a single person.

Allotments have huge potential value as sources for home-grown fruit and vegetables, and it is an enormous shame that so many have been built on. The National Trust contributed to a revival by creating 1,200 new allotments on its land between 2009 and 2012, a popular scheme which lets people grow their own food in beautiful surroundings. Sixty-one of the allotments were on Dinefwr Home Farm in Llandeilo. An allotment association, Cymdeithas y Dalar, was formed there in 2007 but it took more than 18 months for planning permission to be granted for the allotments and for a tenancy agreement to be drawn up. At first the planning authority said no buildings could be constructed, but by 2014 there were two polytunnels and a composting toilet. The absence of any nearby toilets had prevented many gardeners from spending as much time on their plots as they really wanted.

Despite unmet demand for food-growing spaces, Eric Pickles MP, the UK government's Secretary of State for Communities and Local Government, began in 2012 to consider abolishing the legal requirement for local councils to provide allotments. He was still 'considering' in 2014. The incipient threat highlights the vulnerability of council-owned allotments, and thus of the food grown on them, to any change in their legal status imposed by Parliament.

For the sake of future nutrition, green areas in towns and cities should be retained and protected. They have an important role supplying food to local urban populations.

EITHER FOOD OR FUEL

As fossil oil diminishes, and the money to buy it disappears even faster, the energy-hungry look to biomass crops grown for their energy value. Yet the supply of biomass will be severely restricted, because good soil is finite and declining every year. This soil must support both biomass crops and food crops. It follows that as biomass occupies more land, the acreage for food production has to fall.

Oilseed rape, corn and sunflowers are already popular crops for biodiesel, although generally the yield per hectare is increased artificially with synthetic fertilisers. The UK could not both feed the population and grow enough oil crops to keep its vehicles on the road. A typical diesel-engined car doing 12,000 miles a year would require about 2.8 acres of oil crop to fuel it. The UK had 35.0 million licensed motor vehicles in 2013, up from 34.4 million in 2010. One in three was diesel-engined.[8] If they travelled 12,000 miles a year, they would need biofuel produced from nearly 33 million acres (32 million acres in 2010). Thirty three million acres is 51,042 square miles, more than England's 50,356 square miles. So even if biodiesel became a mainstream fuel, it would support only a small fraction of the vehicles which were on Britain's roads in 2014.

The tropical perennial oilseed plant *Jatropha curcas*, a native of Mexico and Central America, is another possibility. *Jatropha curcas* has the potential to yield heavily in hot climates with moderate rainfall of about 31 to 32 inches or 800 millimetres. One hectare can provide up to 500 litres of oil after the first year, rising to a maximum of 2,500 litres or so after three years. India has a major programme to plant *Jatropha curcas*, especially in areas at risk from soil erosion and desertification. The oil can replace fossil diesel, and in addition the plant has other benefits. The oil cake residues make a fertiliser rich in nitrogen, phosphorous and potassium, the leaves repel some insect pests, the bark yields a blue dye, and most parts have medicinal uses, for skin ailments, sores, rheumatism and haemorrhoids. The plant should be an important source of oil in future, although most yields would be much lower than the maxima suggested by the crop's supporters, because of diseases and less-than-ideal growing conditions. A top yield of 2,500 litres of oil per hectare equates to 15.7 barrels of petroleum.

The still-rising annual consumption of oil makes the task of substitution harder. In 2005, the world used about 30.3 billion barrels of oil, equating to unrealistically high yields of Jatropha oil from a land area of about 19.3 million square kilometres, more than the whole area of Russia, the world's largest country, which extends over 17 million square kilometres. In 2010 world oil consumption was higher at 32 billion barrels.[9] On the same basis of impossibly high and uniform Jatropha yields, the theoretical land area needed would be 20.4 million square kilometres. Come 2014, consumption had increased to over 33.4 billion barrels. Replacing this with Jatropha oil would demand top yields from 21.3 million square kilometres, almost one-seventh of the entire land area of the world. The fact that oil use is still rising, when it should be declining towards a level that could be sustained for a few decades while alternative, sustainable technologies are introduced, indicates that no authority has the power to engineer, worldwide, a soft landing from oil dependency.

Gordon Brown, when Chancellor of the UK, included a biofuel promise in his Pre-Budget Statement in December 2005, which stated that, by 2010-11, 5% of the volume of transport fuels used in the UK had to be made from renewable sources and that biofuel manufacturers, whether making biodiesel or bioethanol,[10] should receive special capital allowances to encourage construction of plants. By 2011 the intended financial support for biofuel projects had been scaled back to competitive grants awarded by the Big

Lottery Fund within the National Lottery,[11] although publicly funded grants of at least 30% were available for new recharging or refuelling stations for vehicles powered by electricity, hydrogen, biofuels and, somewhat controversially, natural gas.[12]

Biofuels could help us to manage the essential transition from energy profligacy to parsimony, but the reality of limited – and declining – agricultural land means that we cannot grow as much fuel as the world currently uses, and at the same time produce enough food to prevent widespread hunger. Fertile land is the key to future survival, and competition for it will intensify.

Shortages of fresh water, and of fossil-fuel dependent fertilisers and pesticides, will mean lower crop yields per hectare. Labour-intensive hoeing and companion planting or permaculture can come to the rescue, but if workers were properly paid, food prices would soar, beyond the pockets of swathes of the population. The Cuban-style solution would be to teach everyone to grow their own fruit and veg, to keep pigs and poultry in gardens, to capture water in barrels and mini reservoirs. The North Korean-type of response could be to enforce minimal rations, to use food as a form of social control.

Access to land is a huge hurdle. In an age of scarcity, the concept of land as private property means that it is held primarily for its capital value, not for its social utility. Intending farmers need deep pockets to buy a farm directly. Solutions to the impasse are starting to appear: community supported agriculture, community land trusts, allotments, even guerrilla gardening, whereby clandestine gardeners plant and maintain unused plots of land, but the scale of these responses is way too small.

COMMUNITY OWNERSHIP

So far in the UK, community land trusts have prioritised the construction of homes to buy or rent at prices affordable for people on low to moderate incomes. Community agriculture is in its early days, and its expansion is restricted by minimal resources.

Tablehurst and Plaw Hatch Community Farm is one of the oldest ventures, dating from 1995. These are two farms near the boundary between East and West Sussex, one at Forest Row, the other at Sharpthorne. Both farms are about 200 acres, both have a farm shop, and are run biodynamically, a holistic system of organic farming in sympathy with the whole environment. A co-operative of some 500 members owns the farm businesses, while St Anthony's Trust, a charity investing in biodynamic farms and training centres, has owned the farmland and buildings since 2005.[13]

Over in Gloucestershire, Stroud Community Agriculture Ltd, which started as a project in 2001, leases two farms with a total of 45 acres and supplies produce to members.[14] Up in Shropshire near Market Drayton, Fordhall Farm has about 8,000 owners who all chipped in to buy this well-known tenanted organic farm to prevent the land from being sold for development. The farmers, brother and sister Ben and Charlotte Hollins, mounted a successful campaign to save the farm, where their late father Arthur had been a pioneer organic farmer of the modern era. Fund raising enabled the Fordhall Community Land Initiative, an industrial and provident society, to buy the farm in July 2006.

Since 2011, on twenty two acres of organic land at Chew Magna, between Bath and Bristol, the not-for-profit organisation which runs The Community Farm produces vegetables on land owned by farmer Luke Hassell. Even newer is the initiative to buy Rush Farm at Stockwood, Worcestershire, where some early episodes of *The Archers* were recorded. The farm belonged to a friend of the late Godfrey Baseley, the originator of the long-running radio serial broadcast by the BBC since May 29th 1950. Stockwood Community Benefit Society set about finding shareholders to buy the 150-acre organic, biodynamic farm, and in 2013 the purchase was in progress. Investors could buy between 100 and 20,000 £1 shares – and by the end of 2013 there was enough to buy the farm and its associated rural business park. Small steps, but steps no less.

MIXED FARMING FOR THE FUTURE

Mixed farming – the production of livestock and crops on the same farm, the crops rotated to prevent soil exhaustion, and manure from the livestock spread back on the land as fertiliser – is more sustainable than intensive monocultures, but in industrial countries has been out of fashion for half a century. If we are to feed ourselves successfully, a combination of mixed farming and fruit-and-vegetable gardening will have to return. Livestock on mixed farms, such as oxen and horses, provide energy to pull implements and carts. Mixed farming, using small hedged fields to help prevent soil erosion, protects the ground. The Earth's soils are being destroyed by desertification, nutrient leaching, loss of organic matter, flooding, over-use, urban development. Each year in China, for example, 2,500 more square kilometres turn to desert.[15] The impacts are huge. On the Tibetan Plateau, the glacier at the headwaters of the Yellow River shrank by 77% between 1966 and 2014. The headwaters of the Yangtse and Lancang rivers, also on the plateau, are similarly affected by glacier disappearance. Where the glaciers once were, grassland appeared, but it has been eaten by prairie dogs, whose population exploded. The prairie dogs ate the plains bare, leaving unprotected soil. Now two-thirds of the headwater grasslands have suffered severe desertification.[16]

In the world's forests, felling of mature trees exposes soil to run-off, and also exposes it to sunlight which dries out the forest floor, making it more susceptible to fires. More than 12,000 square miles of Amazon rain forest are destroyed every year, an area exceeding one two-hundredth of the entire Amazon basin, disappearing every year. Felling the trees means less plant life to absorb carbon dioxide. The disappearance of the Amazon forest also has desperate consequences for the indigenous population, fewer than 250,000 of whom survive. A vital knowledge base of plants and their nutritional and medicinal properties vanishes with them. As Raintree Nutrition

Inc[17] pointed out, "Each time a Rainforest medicine man dies, it is as if a library has burned down."

Paradoxically and dangerously, once deforestation has reduced carbon dioxide absorption and contributed to higher temperatures, the remaining plants may emit more carbon dioxide than they absorb – a possible example of positive feedback taking the system away from stability.[18]

FOOD SECURITY

Food security –for whom?

In so far as they are concerned at all, governments generally prioritise food for their own populations. This leads to land grabs, export bans and other measures like quotas and taxes. FAO, the Food and Agriculture Organization of the United Nations, listed many incidents of export bans between 2007 and 2010, in its research working paper no.32.[19] India, Vietnam and Egypt were among countries to ban rice exports, Pakistan banned wheat exports and Russia put a block on the export of major grain crops.

If only all governments were implementing policies to raise the quality of soils, to focus on improving access to land for small-to-medium scale farmers, to encourage local consumption, and to spread knowledge of permaculture as a sustainable farming system. If only they co-operated more to improve food supply to everyone. But they rarely do.

In 'developed' economies like the UK, food security has been given low priority, the argument being that food is just one category of goods and services in international trade and so does not need to be prioritised. Margaret Beckett MP, who at the time was Secretary of State for Environment, Food and Rural Affairs, expressed this view in 2005. On July 6th that year she was giving evidence to the House of Lords Select Committee on the European Union, and in reply to a question[20] from Lord Christopher, who asked: "Have you got in the context of the WTO *[World Trade Organization]* discussions anybody working at all on the issue of food security, certainly for the United Kingdom?" Mrs Beckett said:

> "We have not got people working on what we might call food security as such, not least because, I am not sure how long it is, but it is certainly many decades, more than a hundred years, probably a couple of hundred years at least, since the United Kingdom has been totally self-sufficient in food. We have long been a trading nation, and very proud to be so, and, in consequence, a nation that imported food, among other things, from elsewhere."

She continued, as if trying to soften the starkness of the admission that no one in DEFRA (the Department for Environment, Food and Rural Affairs) was concerned with food security:

> "What we are certainly doing though, and we are putting quite a lot of effort into, is encouraging local sourcing, which is a different way of approaching the same problem, and for a variety of different reasons. We think genuinely there is very high quality of British food available, but there is much benefit, not least when one considers food miles, in encouraging people to source produce locally, and so we are continuing to look at that, including working within the public sector to encouraging more local sourcing. Therefore, we are addressing it from that point of view really rather than from an abstract concept of food security. I know that was part of the consideration when the Common Agricultural Policy was first set up for Europe as a whole, not least in the aftermath of food shortages during the war, but I think if you asked us now where do we see the security concerns, it would be more in terms of energy security and indeed climate security. The big risks that we see today stem from the impact of climate."

So the Department for Environment, Food and Rural Affairs saw energy and climate insecurity as threats, but not food insecurity. The advice to source locally when feasible was an avoidance of the responsibility to have a proper food security plan, and in practice meant nothing definite at all.

There was no real change in this perception by 2011. James Paice MP, in a written reply in January 2011 to a question from Tim Farron MP, said:

"The Government have no plans to hold reserve stocks of food. In the UK Food Security Assessment [*published in August 2009 and updated in January 2010*] DEFRA assesses that the UK enjoys a high level of food security, and we are continuously reviewing our evidence base to maintain this situation."[21]

DEFRA's UK Food Security Assessment[22] is somewhat Panglossian in tone, carrying the assumption that food supplies to British households would continue to be plentiful, and that those households would continue to be able to afford adequate diets. Food production at present levels depends on copious use of manufactured fertilisers and pesticides, which in turn consume fossil oil and gas. The food security assessment document states confidently (in box 10) that "Global proven reserves of crude oil and natural gas are rising". The evidence for this assertion is the data published by the Energy Information Administration of the USA, which has its own agendas. Citing the World Bank, the assessment claims:

"The existence of ample (and growing) reserves, and a history of significant improvements in the technology with which resources are found and extracted, suggests that supply will continue to rise in pace with demand."

However in the same paragraph in box 10 we read:

"True resource exhaustion is unlikely not least because, as resources become scarcer, their prices rise, consumption declines, and alternatives that once may have been uneconomic are substituted for the scarce (and expensive) commodity."

So reserves are both growing and become scarcer, but the authors say there is no need to worry because when one energy source is used up, we will just find another one. This seems rather loose thinking on which to base the food security of a nation.

Food security concerns receded from the news agenda in 2014 and into 2015, because the prices of most foodstuffs were sliding, despite the ticking up, up, up of the world population. Lack of effective demand is a significant cause of lower prices, and a consequence of colossal wealth inequality. When 85 individuals have as much wealth as half the world's population, as Oxfam reported[23] in January 2014, demand is horribly skewed. There are only so many steaks, loaves, and bowls of muesli, even bottles of champagne and plates of caviar, that the 85 can swallow, despite their £ billions. As for half the world's population, on October 20th 2014 they totalled 3.634 billion, just 10 day later, more than 3.635 billion, and they could eat a lot if only they had the resources – land, water, seeds, money – to grow, raise or buy it. So often, they do not. The impoverishment of the masses is the hallmark of the early 21st century. To try and maintain consumption, individuals, organisations and countries borrow – and the debts they accumulate hang suspended, threateningly, above their collective heads. If enough cannot repay, the financial network collapses as it did in 2007 and 2008 when low-income American mortgagees *en masse* could not make repayments. Then the dominos fell.

Lack of purchasing power has contributed to an overall easing of key commodity prices. The next chart illustrates the easing between 2010 and 2014.

Chart 4: Commodities in a time of deflation

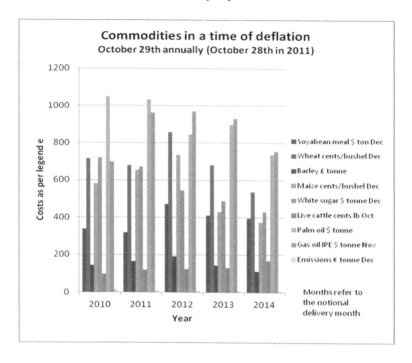

Source: Archived commodity prices published daily by the Financial Times. Original data from Thomson Reuters.

The 'liberation' of oil and gas from shales by fracking pushed fossil energy prices downwards, and this at least provided a temporary lifebelt for shoppers. A long-term fix it is not, because of the colossal costs of extraction and the environmental dangers.

The actuary Gail Tverberg has studied commodity prices for several years. She says:

"If commodity prices drop for any reason – even if it is because a debt bubble is popping – it is going to affect how much companies are willing to produce. There is going to be a tendency to cut back in new production. If prices drop too far, it is even possible that some companies will leave the market altogether." [24]

Governments with fossil fuel industries on their territories also suffer. If industries are not profitable, they do not pay taxes, and resources for public services are strangled.[25] Politicians have to walk the tightrope between promises to keep their voters reasonably content and obtaining the money to secure that contentment. The typical politician in a 'democracy' generally dares not introduce radical measures that would immediately turn a majority of voters against him or occasionally her, even if that means ignoring dangers lurking beyond the time horizon of the next election. The UK government is not sure what to do about debt, or energy, or food security, or climate change, or how to link climate policy with food policy, or agriculture policy, or transport policy, or industry policy, and the financially challenged circumstances mean that decisions are likely to remain short-term – and timid.

The timidity is a result of the restricted freedom that politicians often claim to labour under, because of the international groups and accords to which their nations belong. In the UK, politicians have manipulated membership of the European Union to reject moves towards a sustainable future. This became clear on reading, to give one example, the government's reasons for rejecting proposals from local authorities in England for green innovations under the 2007 Sustainable Communities Act. The proposals were published in December 2009 and the government's response – after the change of administration from Labour to Coalition in May 2010 – appeared in December 2010.[26] West Lancashire District Council had proposed that the government should lobby the European Union for changes to the Treaty of Rome, to allow councils to favour local suppliers and local workers when deciding on contracts. Government rejected this as contrary to the EU requirement for non-discrimination, and on the topic of local food commented that it would not be permissible for local authorities to take account of food miles, or environmental impacts, when awarding contracts, although this seems to have been a mistaken interpretation of the regulations.

Environmental impacts <u>can</u> be taken account in procurement decisions throughout the European Union, as the extract below, from the European Commission's 'Frequently asked questions on green public procurement' [27] makes fairly clear:

> "Contracting authorities can take life-cycle costs into account where the award criterion of most economically advantageous tender (MEAT) is applied. The application of life-cycle costing forms a central part of the approach to GPP *[green public procurement]* promoted by the European Commission and many Member States. It is important when assessing life-cycle costs to apply a methodology which is transparent and allows for the equal treatment of all tenderers."

Life cycle costs originally included the original investment, operating costs, maintenance costs, and the costs of decommissioning and disposal. The addition of environmental costs is a noticeable nod towards green anxieties, but only costs which can be quantified and given a monetary value are counted. The monetary value is only a guess, what 'the market' is prepared to pay. Acidification, eutrophication, greenhouse gas emissions, loss of agricultural land...: how can anyone put a financial value on these 'externalities', as the environmental consequences of economic activity are labelled? The very word 'externality' makes the consequences appear peripheral to the real business of exploiting the environment and everything – and increasingly nearly everyone – alive in it. The European Commission explains:

> "To be introduced into an 'accounting' LCC *[life cycle costs]* process, environmental costs must be expressed in monetary terms. In other words, environmental costs should be quantified and monetised so they can be considered as an additional cost input in a LCC analysis." [28]

What sort of Green is this approach? It appears to be an anaemic Bright Green, to draw on the Typologies of Green outlined in Chapter 1. The trouble is that Bright Greens subordinate the environment to the financial system which people have constructed, although humanity and its creations are components of the environment, not its managers.

In the UK, most of the 'sustainability' proposals which the 2010-15 government opted to support were also variants of Bright Green, technical tweaks with scant cost implications, such as allowing local authorities to sell electricity generated from renewable sources. Radical shifts are not permitted, and this makes the task of preparing for a scarce-energy future all but impossible, like a sailor prevented from leaping into a lifeboat because he is shackled to the deck of a sinking ship.

The inflexible political philosophy of capitalism has become so dominant that it limits the range of policy options. The report *Foresight: The Future of Food and Farming,* published by the UK government's Office for Science in January 2011, contains several unchallenged assumptions, regarded as 'common sense', including corporate control of the food chain, free trade as an unquestioned good, rising prosperity around the world, continued major migration away from rural areas into cities, and the dominance of the global market over community and national priorities.

The report accepts constraints on food production such as water scarcity, land degradation, climate change and high energy costs, but assumes that the free market[29] is the universal solution. The contradictions in the text included this:

> "Food security is best served by fair and fully functioning markets and not by policies to promote self-sufficiency. However, placing trust in the international system does not mean relinquishing a country's sovereignty, rights and responsibilities to provide food for its population."
> -- *Foresight: The Future of Food and Farming*, p.19

This quotation from *Foresight: The Future of Food and Farming* seems a statement of intent without any policy to give it meaning. The statement supposes that markets are fair, and that they will achieve social objectives if only they are left alone. The report

187

proposes (p.13) a ban on food export bans, which I interpret as privileging the interests of commodity trading companies above populations in need of food.

Another oxymoron relates to globalised sustainability.

> "A globalised food system also improves the global efficiency of food production by allowing bread-basket regions to export food to less favoured regions."
>
> -- *Foresight: The Future of Food and Farming*, p.13

Huge trade flows over long distances, eating up fossil energy and emitting greenhouse gases with abandon, are surely the antithesis of sustainability. The "establishment of development corridors linked to major ports" are proposed (p.17) as "a very effective way of stimulating local economies". The greenwash term "local economies" really means "corporate opportunities". The proposal (p.17) to strengthen rights to land and natural resources, such as water, fisheries and forests, means to endow private ownership rights over vital, communal resources. To this end, business and financial reform should "facilitate entrepreneurship in the food production sector", which would "increase food production, household revenue, livelihood diversification and the strength of rural economies". How would entrepreneurship improve sustainability? No answers.

The report advocates reducing food waste, estimated at 30% of production, but has little to say about the links between long supply chains and waste. Indeed, the presupposition that long supply chains are efficient (and sustainable) permeates the text.

The next quotation sums up the fashion to say that sustainability is important but must not be allowed to get in the way of making money:

> "Future reform of international institutions such as the World Trade Organization cannot ignore the issues of sustainability and climate

change. But there is the risk that allowing sustainability to be reflected in trade rules may lead to environmental protectionism."
-- *Foresight: The Future of Food and Farming*, p.20

So environmental protectionism is bad? Yes, it must be that it limits corporate profits. Of course. On page 21 of the report there is more about leaving it all to the market: "there does not seem to be an argument for intervention to influence the number of companies in each area or how they operate". What about cutting greenhouse gas emissions? The "creation of market incentives" (p.29) should sort it out, at least in the view of the authors.

The big solution to world hunger contained in the report's pages is "sustainable intensification". Another oxymoron, but presented as advice to government.

When thinking like this prevails, calling for more of the same failing, exploitative practices, it is tempting (and practical) to retreat into the garden and grow vegetables. But it's not enough.

Back in 1965 Georg Borgstrom, then professor of food science at Michigan State University in the USA, wrote *The Hungry Planet: the Modern World at the Edge of Famine*. In this book, very relevant today, he wrote:[30]

"In order to tackle the great problems of our time we have to rid ourselves of one-eyed technological thinking. We have every reason to admire the scientific knowledge and technical skill which lie behind the space accomplishments of the postwar period, so much more so because this research has widened the boundaries of our knowledge on many important points. But the belief that this is the only way to acquire this information is the tragic mistake of our time. In many cases it is clearly the most expensive way. We have followed the path of least resistance – it is easier to win the ears of the politicians with the new and the fantastic. But the day of reckoning will dawn, and it is probably not so far away, when science and technology will be held responsible before mankind. Men of all nations will then become aware that the spectacular promises given by dam constructors, plant breeders, soil scientists, and chemists have not been fulfilled."

189

The evidence that I have tried to present in this book suggests to me that we should take more responsibility ourselves for producing at least some of our food. Looking down from a flat in London's Whitechapel recently, over the back gardens of maisonettes, it seemed that most were used for leisure, but even in the heart of the city there were some where vegetables and herbs were flourishing in pots, tubs and raised beds. We need to press local authorities and socially responsible landowners for more allotments where people can grow their own food. We have to demand local food from supermarkets and support shops which specialise in local food. If we eat meat, we should favour cuts from animals reared naturally and preferably organically, and we should be willing to eat meat less often.

If we concentrate on increasing the number and range of plants in our diets, on growing more of our own food, on making soil-improving compost from plant wastes, and on favouring local producers of foods that we cannot supply ourselves, we would be helping to save fuel, to trim carbon emissions, and at the same time to improve our own health and well-being.

NETWORKS OF DIVERSITY

Local community activism is a way of exerting at least a modicum of control over a political world which seems in 2015 like an out-of-control locomotive careering who knows where. As if the uncertainties of conflicts all around the world were not enough, in September 2014 the UK faced the Scots' vote on independence after 307 years of union. This union has lasted longer than the Irish-UK union of 1801 to 1922, but has been damaged by an English predilection to conflate 'England' with the 'United Kingdom', a perspective which forms a barrier to the development of an English parliament and a federal government which could be more resilient over the longer term. Fifty-five per cent of the almost 85% of Scots who voted chose to reject independence -- an apparent failure, but membership of the pro-independence Scottish National Party continued to surge afterwards. Despite Scotland's vote to remain in the UK, the future form of UK government is not at all certain. Boundaries are not for ever, and treating them as permanent guarantees of independence conveys a false sense of security. Local self-sufficiency by itself is not enough to create any stability, but in combination with networks of collaborative and federal organisations is a source of at least some personal independence. A future like this, a new form of post-industrial society, is often debated by supporters of low-impact development and 'One Planet' living, but rarely by mainstream politicians, who either see nothing to worry about, or are anxious to avoid alarming the voters.

Business as usual, only more so, remains the dominant paradigm of in-power politicians and civil servants. 'Growth' is the watchword, and the quest for growth is a significant force behind the controversial Transatlantic Trade and Investment Partnership (TTIP), not yet in being at the time of writing, but looming.

TTIP, a proposed 'open market' trade deal between the USA and the European Union, has near miraculous status in the minds of its proponents. Take this paean from an EU question-and-answer document:[31]

"European companies, workers and citizens would benefit enormously from a more open US market. The EU has many highly competitive firms producing top quality products and services, including many world leaders and top brands. In agriculture, for example, US plant health regulations ban European apples, while their food safety rules make it illegal to import many European cheeses. Getting rid of tariffs and other barriers to trade will enable European producers to sell more to the Americans: that is good for business and good for jobs. Removing EU barriers to US products and investment will mean more choice and lower prices for people here in Europe. What is clear is that both sides will gain from further opening up their markets to trade and investment. It will be a win-win situation."

Win win for whom, the reader wonders. In 2013 the European Commission asked the Centre for Economic Policy Research (CEPR)[32]

191

to investigate the pros and cons of TTIP, and the CEPR's figures indicated financial benefits. As far as the EU Commission was concerned, the CEPR was likely to be a safe pair of hands, and so it proved. The centre receives funding from a long list of banks, including central banks and commercial banks from around the world, and calls upon a network of academic economists to lead research projects.

Academic economists have long prioritised theory over the messy reality of the real world. Particularly, they are reluctant to worry about resource unavailability, on the basis that if one commodity is unattainable, clever humans will find another to substitute. The CEPR asked if TTIP would result in economic growth, and concluded that yes, it would, and is therefore highly desirable.

TTIP is about 'harmonising' regulations, which tend to slip towards a lowest common denominator, and also about protecting corporations from governments which change – strengthen – the regulatory environment. The protection will be in the Investor State Dispute Settlement (ISDS) system. This means that foreign companies, or multinationals whose operations in a territory are (even if nominally) controlled from outside the borders, are at liberty to sue governments who do anything likely to threaten the future flow of profits. ISDS cases in the TTIP would be heard in secret by a panel of specialist lawyers.

The negotiations for TTIP are proceeding in secret. The EU Commission justifies this as follows:

"For trade negotiations to work and succeed, you need a certain degree of confidentiality, otherwise it would be like showing the other players one's cards in a card game."[33]

This is a weak argument. A trade agreement with the potential profoundly to change European societies – weaker environmental protection, lower wages resulting from more ferocious competition, the likely introduction of technologies such as seeds-and-chemicals packages, to which many people object – is rather more serious than a game of gin rummy or whist.

TTIP may be profitable for the world's big corporations, their owners, lawyers and advisers, but the very concept of ISDS, privileging capital above all other considerations, is profoundly regressive. There are voices against TTIP, although they lack the clout of TTIP's cheerleaders. The Austrian Foundation for Development Research, Vienna produced a report called 'Assessing the Claimed Benefits of the Transatlantic Trade and Investment Partnership', [34] which is more balanced and draws out disadvantages, such as the compensation payments governments would have to make to corporations if they strengthened regulation, the loss of income to governments when tariffs are abolished, welfare costs if workers become unemployed, and lower tax revenues. The report concludes:

> "Last but not least, an investor-to-state dispute settlement mechanism, if included in TTIP, could lead to compensation payments by governments and have a disciplining effect on future regulation in the public interest. A qualified public debate on the need for such an arbitration mechanism as currently proposed, and a discussion about alternative forms of international investment arbitration, which is both transparent and equilibrated in its treatment of investors' rights and the prerogatives of public policy, is urgently needed." [35]

The Centre for Economic Policy Research, happily assuming minimal drawbacks, reckoned that TTIP would bring €119 billion to the EU and €95 billion to the USA, which would equate to €545 for a family of four in Europe and €655 for a family in the USA. Equivalence is not actual income, though, and it is possible that families would not see any of the claimed benefits. The aim is not to make all families more prosperous, but to open doors for business. Even before TTIP, tariffs between the EU and the USA average less than 3% -- and even more to the point, at least a third of transatlantic trade is intra-company, i.e. companies sending their own goods from one side of the Atlantic to the other, for whom the removal of tariffs has immediate cash flow benefits.

The North American Free Trade Agreement (NAFTA) has lessons for TTIP. NAFTA, a deal between the USA, Canada and Mexico introduced in 1994, has increased the power of major corporations, free to move capital and production wherever they want, a freedom which intensifies job insecurity and damages conditions for workers. Free markets, however, are still in vogue among the upper echelons of governments around the world.

The world's unfettered free markets are hardly bastions of ethics. The dry-sounding 'Changes stemming from improved comparability of Gross National Income measurement', published by the UK's Office for National Statistics on May 16th 2014, includes these startling, shocking sentences:

> "...illegal activities (e.g. prostitution and production of drugs) fall within the production boundary of national accounts. The sources and methods used need to be reviewed in order to ensure that illegal activities are properly included in the national accounts. The UK already includes estimates in the national accounts for smuggling of alcohol and tobacco, so this reservation will be addressed by including prostitution and drugs within the national accounts framework."

The announcement was one of a number from statistics offices in the European Union, as members moved to harmonise a way of inflating economic growth by estimating the amounts changing hands illegally! Criminal activities such as drug pushing are good for the numbers, because buyers who are addicted will pay the price asked, even if they have to turn to more crime to get the money. Governments evidently value crime as a pillar of economic output.

Is this the end of ethics in government? How can politicians expect people to behave ethically when criminal activities are valued for contributing to national income? The European Commission pushed member states down this road when in December 2013 it included the proposals in the 'European System of National and Regional Accounts'. This shows the Commission's priorities – economic growth above all other considerations. Maybe the European Union is not such a force for social good after all.

Complaints in the media were muted and, it seems, short-lived. For the mainstream media too, the imperative for economic growth is unquestioned. Nearly all activities, including childcare -- parents paying other people to look after their children while they work to earn the money to pay the childminders - have already been monetised, prompting the powers-that-be, in a desperate gamble, to co-opt the underworld.

The UK's boost to gross domestic product from the addition of illegal activities was thought to be £10 billion, about £155 per man, woman and child. The £10 billion figure is, of course, only a guess as no one really knows. The figure is probably inaccurate as well as reprehensible.

'GREEN AND PLEASANT LAND' MEETS 'LIMITS TO GROWTH'

Limits to Growth, a book by Donella Meadows, Dennis Meadows, Jorgen Randers and William Behrens III, powerfully explaining that continuous growth is impossible on a planet of fixed size, from which energy and mineral resources are being consumed vastly faster than their natural rate of formation, was published in 1972.

At the end of the same decade in 1979, sociologist Howard Newby's *Green and Pleasant Land? Social Change in Rural England*, was published by Hutchinson, and a Pelican paperback followed in 1980.

Howard Newby's basic assumptions fitted the new Thatcherite spirit of the times. It was of course in 1979 that Margaret Thatcher became prime minister of the United Kingdom. In Newby's view, the future of agriculture was BIG.

"...there is now a general recognition that the accumulation of surpluses in the EEC will only be finally removed if farm prices are so low that the less efficient producers are forced out of existence and output is concentrated on those farms with the necessary capital

195

resources to increase productivity and yields still further. This will require a significant drop in the number of both farmers and farm workers within the industry, yet the social costs arising from a politically popular reform of the CAP *[Common Agricultural Policy]* have barely been considered in the public debate which has arisen since Britain entered the EEC.

"The only sustained and articulate opposition to this trend has come from the environmental lobby, which has not only been highly critical of the effects of modern agricultural practice on the ecology of the countryside, but has also called into question some of the basic assumptions of agricultural policy – such as its measure of 'efficiency' – and presented an apocalyptic vision of the future if current developments are allowed to continue."
-- *Green and Pleasant Land*, Pelican edition p.270

In Howard Newby's opinion, that apocalyptic vision was exaggerated. While some forecasters predicted a world energy crisis, and while such a crisis could happen,

"...the proportion of petrochemical production used on Britain's farms is sufficiently small, and the likelihood of agriculture being given priority in any system of allocation so great, that only moderate adjustments ought to be necessary – a small reversal of the trend towards specialisation, perhaps, though not necessarily any reduction in scale...

"...The most likely future is therefore 'more of the same' – the continuation and extension of the kinds of changes which we have observed in agriculture since the war. The numbers of both farmers and farm workers will continue to decline and, although many small farms will survive, the industry will be dominated, in terms of both output and hired manpower, by a comparatively small number of very large farms, many of which will emerge under the aegis of outside capital investment."
-- *Green and Pleasant Land*, Pelican edition, pps. 270 and 271

The 1970s and 1980s were the decades when transnational financial and industrial corporations took ready advantage of swift access to capital to implement technological changes which increased their market power. Howard Newby, whose later career[36] was as a university vice-chancellor, regarded science as a continuous source of problem solving, and 'limits to growth' did not impact on his argument in any central way. His thinking is not too different from many assumptions still widely held today, the central one being confidence that science will find a way.

I do not know if Howard Newby had read *Limits to Growth* when he wrote *Green and Pleasant Land*, but if he had done so, he would have been aware of this conclusion:

"If the present growth trends in world population, industrialization, pollution, food production and resource depletion continue unchanged, the limits to growth on this planet will be reached sometime within the next one hundred years. The most probable result will be a rather sudden and uncontrollable decline in both population and industrial capacity."
-- *Limits to Growth*, by Donella Meadows, Dennis Meadows, Jorgen Randers and William Behrens III, Universe Books, 1972, p23.[37]

One hundred years is no more than three or four generations. By 1972 I had graduated. In 2072 my current grandchildren would be 66, 71 and 75. The thought of them facing a sudden and uncontrollable population decline, similar to or worse than the bubonic plagues which terrorised the medieval world, is deeply worrying. We are in 2015 approaching half way between 1972 and 2072, but the world's powerful decision-makers have by and large ignored the red traffic lights illuminated in *Limits to Growth*.

People say 'I'll carry on flying all the time I can', 'I need a car, there's no public transport round here', 'My child's school insists on this new expensive uniform, I've no option but to buy it', and in truth the populations of wealthy countries are enmeshed in consumption networks from which escape is difficult. Consumer spending has become the bedrock of the economy, to such an extent that it can seem unpatriotic to scale back consumption to a sustainable level, using no more than a fair share of the Earth's resources instead of two-and-a half to three times more, as in the UK, or four times more, as in the USA.[38]

Over-consumption of irreplaceable resources was not an important issue for Howard Newby, but he was in a large majority at the time, and this sanguine view is still widespread today. The authors of *Limits to Growth* were whistling into an offshore wind, and although the return echo is louder now, it is too easily ignored. Perhaps, unlike the late Donella Meadows, we find it hard to think in terms of complex systems. It is easier to frame issues narrowly. Take a proposed new road which would destroy ancient woodland. Easy, change the route! But this is very narrow thinking, which excludes fundamental issues such as 'Why do we need a new road?' and 'Can we reduce the movement of people and goods?' GDP and jobs are the big hurdles. A new road creates construction activity and jobs, which give the economy a short-term boost even if hastening its eventual demise.

Against the rapid cycles of statistical reporting and government elections, the protection of ecological systems continues to have low priority, and this will be the case until 'the economy' stops meaning the pursuit of financial profit and the attempted domination of the natural world, and transforms into an understanding of ecological systems in which humans are participants, but not aspiring, delusional controllers.

It may take a few decades of unstoppable climate change before such a radical semantic shift becomes the new common sense.

---

[1]'An examination of falling real wages 2010 to 2013', Office for National Statistics, January 31st 2014, www.ons.gov.uk/ons/rel/elmr/an-examination-of-falling-real-wages/2010-to-2013/art-an-examination-of-falling-real-wages.html#tab-Long-run-trends-in-real-wage-growth-

[2] 'Urban cultivation in allotments maintains soil qualities adversely affected by conventional agriculture' by Jill L Edmondson, Zoe G Davies, Kevin J Gaston and Jonathan R Leake, *Journal of Applied Ecology* vol.51 issue 4 pps. 880-889.

[3] *Down to Earth* was published in 1970 by Crosby Lockwood.

[4] 'Britain has only 100 harvests left in its farm soil as scientists warn of growing 'agricultural crisis', by Adam Withnall, October 20th 2014.

[5] Esmée Fairbairn, who died in an air raid in the Second World War, was the wife of Ian Fairbairn, whose company M&G pioneered the unit trust industry in Britain. Ian Fairbairn, and Esmée's sons Paul and Oliver Stobart, set up the fund in her memory.

[6] 25.29 square metres.

[7] One sixty-sixth to one thirty-third of a hectare.

[8] Statistics from Department of Transport's Vehicle Licensing Statistics.

[9] International Energy Agency oil market report, January 18th 2011.

[10] Bioethanol is alcohol produced by fermenting the sugars in plants.

[11] The Big Lottery Fund distributes funds from the National Lottery and from other available sources.

[12] Grant information and funding sources, www.therenewableenergycentre.co.uk, accessed January 18th 2011.

[13] www.tablehurstandplawhatch.co.uk, accessed June 2nd 2014.

[14] Common Wealth by Martin Large, Hawthorn Press, 2010, p.253

[15] Figure from 'Red dust rising' by Mark Lynas in The Ecologist, February 1st 2004.

[16] 'Desertification in China threatens headwaters in the Tibetan Plateau', www.visiontimes.com/2014/03/02/desertification-in-china-threatens-headwaters-in-the-tibetan-plateau.html, March 2nd 2014.

[17] Raintree Nutrition Inc, Carson City, Nevada. www.rain-tree.com/facts.htm

[18] This finding was from the Laboratoire des Sciences du Climat et de l'Environnement in France, in September 2005. Reported on the BBC: 'Heatwave makes plants warm planet', by Richard Black, http://news.bbc.co.uk/1/hi/sci/tech/4269066.stm

[19] 'Food Export Restrictions: Review of the 2007-2010 Experience and Considerations for Disciplining Restrictive Measures' by Ramesh Sharma, FAO Commodity and Trade Policy Research Working Paper no.32, May 2011.

[20] Question 7 in the committee's minutes of evidence for July 6th 2005, www.publications.parliament.uk/pa/ld200506/ldselect/ldeucom/36/5070602.htm, House of Lords Select Committee on the European Union.

[21] Hansard, written answers to questions, Monday January 17th 2011.

[22] 'UK Food Security Assessment: Detailed Analysis', DEFRA, January 2010 update.

[23] Working for the Few: Political capture and economic inequality. Oxfam briefing paper 178 by Ricardo Fuentes-Nieva and Nicholas Galasso, January 2014.

[24] 'Low oil prices: sign of a debt bubble collapse, leading to the end of oil supply?' by Gail Tverberg, September 21st 2014, http://ourfiniteworld.com/2014/09/21/low-oil-prices-sign-of-a-debt-bubble-collapse-leading-to-the-end-of-oil-supply/

[25] Gail Tverberg, as above.

[26] www.communities.gov.uk/documents/communities/pdf/1798995.pdf, 'Decisions on proposals submitted following the 2008 invitation'.

[27] European Commission,
http://ec.europa.eu/environment/gpp/faq_en.htm#general1
[28] European Commission, http://ec.europa.eu/environment/gpp/lcc.htm
[29] The 'free market' in the 21st century is not really free, as John Michael Greer pointed out in *The Ecotechnic Future*, 2009. He wrote (p.65) that it was more a "slanted playing board designed to maximise the flow of wealth to the world's industrial nations and minimize flows in the other direction, it replaced more straightforward forms of colonialism while maintaining unequal patterns of exchange that allow the five per cent of the world's population who live in the United States to use about a third of the world's natural resources".
[30] P.468 of the 1970 printing by Collier Books.
[31] European Commission, http://ec.europa.eu/trade/policy/in-focus/ttip/questions-and-answers/
[32] 'Estimating the Economic Impact on the UK of a Transatlantic Trade and Investment Partnership (TTIP) Agreement between the European Union and the United States'. Final project report by the Centre for Economic Policy Research, March 2013.
[33] European Commission, as above.
[34] 'Assessing the claimed benefits of the Transatlantic Trade and Investment Partnership' by Werner Raza and Bernhard Tröster, Austrian Foundation for Development Research, Vienna, 2014, www.guengl.eu/uploads/plenary-focus-pdf/ASSESS_TTIP.pdf
[35] Part V, Conclusions and policy recommendations,
www2.euromemorandum.eu/uploads/raza_assessing_the_claimed_benefits_of_the_transatlantic_ttip.pdf
[36] Sir Howard Joseph Newby CBE DL, formerly professor of sociology at the University of Essex, was vice-chancellor at the University of Southampton 1994-2001, at the University of the West of England 2006-08 and the University of Liverpool from 2008. In 2014 he announced that he would retire from Liverpool in 2015. He has held many other public appointments, including president of Universities UK 1999-2001 and president, Academy of Social Sciences 2008-13.
[37] *Limits to Growth* is downloadable from www.donellameadows.org/wp-content/userfiles/Limits-to-Growth-digital-scan-version.pdf
[38] Global Footprint Network, www.footprintnetwork.org, accessed January 7th 2015.

FORWARD

Four actions we can all take:

- Insulate our homes to the maximum.
- Grow as many food plants as we can, indoors and out.
- Limit methods of travel powered by fossil fuels.
- Learn a skill which will be in demand in a resource-challenged future – repairing domestic appliances or computers, knitting, carpentry, horticulture, all the practical skills which lost kudos in the age of buy, buy, buy.

All have some adverse implications for any economy which, like the UK's, is so heavily dependent on consumer spending. Once insulation is in place, spending on heating will decline. People growing their own food spend less in supermarkets and shops. Less travel by car, bus, train and plane also feeds through into lower gross domestic product (GDP) per head. The more we can repair and reuse, the less we will need new gadgets.

Governments are terrified of any decline in GDP. A shrinking economy in an indebted nation – and almost all national governments are indebted – makes the debts much harder to repay, and limits the potential to take on new debt. The prospect of a fall in GDP per head raises spectres of lower tax revenues, threatening public spending commitments and promising a spiral of financial decline, into a depression in which populations are impoverished.

Yet if we carry on spending, and borrowing to spend more, we collide sooner with the limits to growth. Reduce consumption, and finite resources will last longer.

The decision to consume less will be forced on us at some point. In the words of actuary Gail Tverberg, explaining the downside of lower oil prices:

> "There is a growing mismatch between what workers in oil importing countries can afford, and the rising real costs of extraction, including

201

associated governmental costs. This has been covered up to date by rising debt, but at some point, it will not be possible to keep increasing the debt sufficiently.

"The timing of collapse may not be immediate. Low oil prices take a while to work their way through the system. It is also possible that the world's financiers will put off a major collapse for a while longer, through more QE [quantitative easing], or more programs related to QE. For example, actually getting money into the hands of customers would seem to be temporarily helpful.

"At some point the debt situation will eventually reach a breaking point. One way this could happen is through an increase in interest rates. If this happens, world economic growth is likely to slow greatly. Oil and commodity prices will fall further. Debt defaults will skyrocket. Not only will oil production drop, but production of many other commodities will drop, including natural gas and coal. In such a scenario, the downslope of all energy use is likely to be quite steep...."
   -- from 'Ten reasons why a severe drop in oil prices is a problem'[1]

The current debt system will collapse sooner or later anyway, so why not take steps to limit our personal dependence on it? Not so much 'stop the world I want to get off' but 'I'm getting off before the world stops'.

It is up to us to persuade governments to plan a steady slowdown, to agree debt cancellations with each other, to require progressive reductions in energy use, and to control the banking industry in the interests of the welfare of their populations. If we can do this, maybe we can achieve a managed slowdown and avoid a violent emergency stop.

However we arrive in the future, in a planned or catastrophic way, we have to look forward to a future with less, the only possible future if we are to have one at all. Even if the systems of which we are part generate new, emergent properties, the finite resources on which we depend will impose limits on our future ambitions. The solution to the Grim Equation is not money, or even technology, but a philosophical shift to place man within the systems of the natural world, instead of trying (and failing) to control them.

---

1   www.ourfiniteworld.com/2014/12/07/ten-reasons-why-a-severe-drop-in-oil-prices-is-a-problem/, by Gail Tverberg.

BIBLIOGRAPHY OF PRINCIPAL BOOKS AND REPORTS CONSULTED IN SOLVING THE GRIM EQUATION

Printed and online articles are referenced in the Endnotes to each chapter

Beck, Ulrich; Giddens, Anthony; Lash, Scott. *Reflexive Modernization: Politics, Tradition and Aesthetics in the Modern Social Order.* Blackwell Publishers, 1994

Blake, Michael. Down to Earth: Real principles for fertiliser practice. Crosby Lockwood, 1970

Borgstrom, Georg. *The Hungry Planet: the Modern World on the Edge of Famine.* Macmillan, 1965

Centre for Economic Policy Research. *Estimating the Economic Impact on the UK of a Transatlantic Trade and Investment Partnership (TTIP) Agreement between the European Union and the United States.* Final project report, March 2013

Cipolla, Carlo M. *The Economic History of World Population.* Penguin Books 1964 edition. First published 1962

Department for Environment, Food and Rural Affairs.
UK Food Security Assessment: Detailed Analysis, update January 2010
Sixty-third Annual Report to Parliament on Smallholdings in England 1 April 2012 – 31 March 2013, February 2014

Department of Energy and Climate Change. *Digest of UK Energy Statistics 2014*, 2014

Department of Trade and Industry. *The Energy Challenge: Energy Review Report*, July 2006

Diamond, Jared. *Collapse: How Societies Choose to Fail or Survive.* Penguin Books 2006. First published 2005 by Viking Penguin and Allen Lane

Ernle, Lord (Prothero, Rowland). *English Farming Past and Present.* Longman's Green & Co, 1927

Friends of the Earth International. *Who Benefits from GM Crops?* 2014

Fuentes-Nieva, Ricardo and **Galasso, Nicholas.** *Working for the Few: Political capture and economic inequality.* Oxfam briefing paper 178, January 2014

Gold, Thomas. *The Deep Hot Biosphere.* Springer, 1999

Government Office for Science, The. *Foresight: The Future of Food and Farming*, 2011

Greer, John Michael. *The Ecotechnic Future.* New Society Publishers, 2009

Heinberg, Richard. *Searching for a Miracle: 'Net Energy' Limits and the Fate of Industrial Society.* Post Carbon Institute and International Forum on Globalization, 2009

Intergovernmental Panel on Climate Change. *Special Report on Carbon Dioxide Capture and Storage.* Working Group III, 2005
Climate Change 2014. Working Group II, March 2014

Irwin, A. *Citizen Science: a study of people, expertise and sustainable development.* Routledge, 1995

King, Stephen D. *When the Money Runs Out: The End of Western Affluence.* Yale University Press, 2013

Large, Martin. *Common Wealth For a free, equal, mutual and sustainable society.* Hawthorn Press, 2010

Macmurray, John. *Conditions of Freedom.* Faber and Faber, 1949

National Geographic Association. *Orbit: NASA Astronauts Photograph the Earth.* 1996

Meadows, Donella H; Meadows, Dennis L; Randers, Jorgen; Behrens, William W III. *Limits to Growth.* Club of Rome, Universe Books, 1972

Newby, Howard. *Green and Pleasant Land: Social Change in Rural England.* Pelican Books edition, 1980

Office for National Statistics. *Annual Survey of Hours and Earnings 2013,* provisional, December 2013
Annual Survey of Hours and Earnings 2014, provisional, November 2014

Pfeiffer, Dale Allen. *Eating Fossil Fuels.* From the Wilderness Publications, 2003

PLATFORM. *Crude Designs: the Rip-off of Iraq's Oil Wealth.* PLATFORM with Global Policy Forum, Institute for Policy Studies, Oil Change International, New Economics Foundation, War on Want, 2005

Raza, Werner and **Tröster, Bernhard.** *Assessing the Claimed Benefits of the Transatlantic Trade and Investment Partnership.* OFSE, the Austrian Foundation for Development Research, 2014

Rietzler, Karolina. *The Role of Scientific Knowledge and Other Knowledge Types in Grassroots Sustainability Initiatives: an exploratory case study of a low impact development eco-village in Wales.* Albert Ludwigs Universität, Freiburg, 2012

Robinson, Arthur B; Baliunas, Sallie L; Soon, Willie; Robinson, Zachary W. *Environmental Effects of Increased Atmospheric Carbon Dioxide.* Oregon Institute of Science and Medicine and George C Marshall Institute, 1998

Rothkopf, David. *Superclass: the Global Power Elite and the World they are Making.* Farrar, Strauss and Giroux, and Little, Brown, 2008

Royal Academy of Engineering, The. *Future Ship Powering Options: Exploring alternative methods of ship propulsion*. 2013

Scarlott, Charles. Limitations to energy use, in Thomas, William L Jr (editor), *Man's Role in Changing the Face of the Earth*. University of Chicago Press, 1956

Schumacher, E F *Small is Beautiful: a Study of Economics as if People Mattered*. Blond & Briggs, 1973

Seymour, John. *The Complete Book of Self-Sufficiency*. Illustrated by Sally Seymour. Faber and Faber, 1976

Siegel, Frederic R. *Countering 21st Century Social-Environmental Threats to Growing Global Populations*. Springer Briefs in Environmental Science, 2015

Simmons, Matthew R. *Twilight in the Desert: the Coming Saudi Oil Shock and the World Economy*. John Wiley & Sons, 2005

Sklair, Leslie. *The Transnational Capitalist Class*. Blackwell Publishers, 2001

Stern, Nicholas. *The Economics of Climate Change*. HM Treasury and the Cabinet Office, January 2006

Sustainable Development Commission, The. *The Role of Nuclear Power in a Low Carbon Economy*, 2006

Tenant Farmers Association. *2020 Vision for Agriculture*. Sponsored by Bircham Dyson Bell, 2010

Thorpe, David. *The 'One Planet' Life: a Blueprint for Low Impact Development*. Routledge, 2015

Treasury, The and **Her Majesty's Revenue & Customs**. *Carbon price floor: support and certainty for low-carbon investment*, December 2010

Tyndall Centre for Climate Change Research. *Climate Change on the Millennium Timescale*. Technical Report 41, 2006

United Nations and **World Bank**
Natural Hazards, UnNatural Disasters: the Economics of Effective Prevention, Overview. 2010

Welsh Government
Renewable Energy, Technical Advice Note 8, 2005
One Wales: One Planet – The Sustainable Development Scheme of the Welsh Assembly Government, May 2009
One planet development practice guide, October 2012
Practice guidance – using the one planet development ecological footprint calculator, October 2012

Wilkinson, Daniel. *Silence on the Mountain: Stories of Terror, Betrayal and Forgetting in Guatemala*. Duke University Press 2004

Woetzel, Jonathan; Mendonca, Lenny; Devan, Janamitra; Negri, Stefano; Yangmel, Hu; Jordan, Luke; Li, Xiujun; Maasry, Alexander; Tsen, Geoff; Yu, Flora. *Preparing for China's urban billion*. McKinsey Global Institute, McKinsey & Company, 2009

World Bank.
Hazards of Nature, Risks to Development: an IEG evaluation of World Bank assistance for natural disasters. April 2006

World Meteorological Association. *Greenhouse Gas Bulletin no.10.* September 2014

MORE USEFUL BOOKS

Carson, Rachel. *Silent Spring*. Houghton Mifflin, 1962

Catton, William R Jr *Bottleneck: Humanity's Impending Impasse*. Xlibris, 2009

Douthwaite, Richard. *The Growth Illusion*. Green Books, 1999

Lovelock, James. *The Revenge of Gaia: Why the Earth is Fighting Back – and How we can still Save Humanity*. Allen Lane, 2006

Madron, Roy and **Jopling, John**. *Gaian Democracies: Redefining Globalisation and People-Power*. Green Books on behalf of Schumacher UK, 2003

Martenson, Chris. *The Crash Course: The Unsustainable Future of Our Economy, Energy and Environment*. John Wiley & Sons Inc, 2011

Meadows, Donella H; Meadows, Dennis L; Randers, Jorgen. *Limits to Growth: The 30-year Update*. Routledge, 2004

Mellanby, Kenneth. *Pesticides and Pollution*. Collins New Naturalist Series, 1967

Milbourne, Paul (editor). *Rural Wales in the Twenty-first Century*. University of Wales, 2011

Mobbs, Paul. *Energy Beyond Oil*. Matador, 2005

Morgan, Tim. *Life After Growth*. Harriman House, 2013

Rihani, Samir. *Complex Systems Theory and Development Practice*. Zed Books, 2002

Roberts, Paul. *The End of Oil: the decline of the petroleum economy and the rise of a new energy order*. Bloomsbury, 2004

Ruppert, Michael C. *Confronting Collapse: The Crisis of Energy and Money in a Post Peak Oil World*. Chelsea Green Publishing Company, 2009

Turchin, Peter and Nefedov, Sergey A. *Secular Cycles*. Princeton University Press, 2009

Urry, John. *Global Complexity*. Polity Press/ Blackwell Publishing, 2003

Wimbush, Paul. *The Birth of an Ecovillage: Adventures in an alternative world*. FeedARead Publishing, 2012

INDEX

215

217

Lightning Source UK Ltd.
Milton Keynes UK
UKOW07f0653100615

253243UK00010B/37/P

9 780993 086298